✝HRİVE

A HANDBOOK FOR CHRISTIAN GROWTH

Growing with
One PLANTs One
discipleship

JAMES H. HALL

Reverend James H. Hall
1411 E. Stoneridge Street
Springfield, Missouri 65803
(417) 833-9052
E-mail: JHHalls@aol.com
Web site: www.newchristian.com

Contents

You are a member of God's eternal family, and you have a mission!

Your second birth was made possible by God's eternal Son Jesus, and you became a child of God – forever, if you continue to daily trust Him with your life here on earth. Daily trust means talking and cooperating with God every day – **embracing His mission** for you in your world.

The lessons in this manual were written to help you clearly hear what God is saying to you through the Bible, His written Word, and to listen intently each day as His Spirit speaks to you. Your spiritual growth will be accompanied by more and more talking to God and depending on Him to help you obey what He tells you. You will also receive assistance in identifying and developing the spiritual gifts placed within you by the Holy Spirit.

But you need more than this handbook and your Bible to maximize your spiritual growth. You need one or more Christian friend(s) who are also growing in their relationship with God through Jesus Christ. You and your friend(s) can discuss what is brought up in the lessons and stated in the Bible passages referenced. Each of you will learn by expressing what you see in those Bible passages, and from hearing what each of you see in the same passages. This will help you understand and obey what God is saying to you. You can celebrate together your progress, encourage each other to keep going, and correct each other when needed.

If you don't have friends to grow with you in this manner, ask God to help you find some – at least one. Meanwhile, go ahead on your own and study the Bible, guided by these sessions, until you find the friend(s) you are praying for.

God has always been happy that you are His child, and He will be even happier as you continue to get to know Him better and better throughout your lifetime. Continue to give your best effort to being diligent in talking with God and listening to Him talk to you. Do your best to continually cooperate with Him by depending on Him to help you know what to do and give you strength to obey.

Study the material well—for your sake, and also to be able to be a helping friend to non-following friends, new believers, and other brothers and sisters in Christ who want to grow – **by using this same material and process with them.**

The big question for you is: Are you:

a) **on the mission** Jesus has assigned you to pursue, or are
b) you merely attempting to maintain enough spiritual activity for God to bless you on earth and take you to heaven when you die?

My prayer is that the experience of growing together with a Christian friend (or friends) will help you stay on mission and effectively:

a) encourage each other and hold each other accountable for applying God's truth to your daily behavior – celebrating and correcting as appropriate, and
b) recruit and assist lost people to follow Jesus with you on earth – so they can go to heaven with you sooner or later.

Eventually we will sit down in eternity and review and give God praise for what He has done through you. Until then, I remain…

Your brother and fellow laborer in the final harvest,

Jim Hall - New Christian Life Ministries

Session Summaries

Phase 2 Prayerful Living (based on the Lord's Prayer)

Contact That Leads to Conduct

Session 6 **Knowing God as Your Father**

The Lord's Prayer gives us a template for praying and living that pleases God. Who you are and what your life means becomes clear when you see God as loving Father and ruling King.

Session 7 **You are a Citizen of Heaven**

"Your kingdom come" is to continue to be your prayer and life's ambition. You live this out and bring God's kingdom to earth now when you live in obedience to God and to His delegated earthly authorities.

Session 8 **Your Daily Supply of Food**

God is your source, and He will faithfully provide for your physical need—if you ask Him to, and if you honor Him with tithes and offerings.

Session 9 **Your Daily Supply of Forgiveness**

God is gracious and is faithful to forgive your sin if you ask Him to—and if you also forgive others—as He has forgiven you!

Session 10 **Freedom through Dependence**

Dependence on God brings freedom from the bondage and heartbreaking consequences of sin. God is always stronger than any temptation, circumstance, or enemy. Therefore, ask God (and act) to help you avoid temptation; and ask Him to rescue you when you are tempted, deceived, or attacked by Satan.

Phase 3 Responsibility

Conduct through Contact

Session 11 **Remembering Jesus Together**

The Lord's Supper (or communion) is a special way commanded by Jesus for you to celebrate with other believers His death and the life He gives by His Spirit living in you. Examine yourself before sharing in this serious celebration. A supplement provides a guide for examining your overall progress in learning to walk with the Lord.

Your Life in Jesus

After waterskiing, Dawson Trotman was tired, but not ready to leave the water. The fun-loving founder of Navigators, an organization built to evangelize the lost and disciple Christians, climbed into a motorboat for a ride. "Daws" asked two girls in the boat if they could swim. One said no, so he sat between them, locking arms with them for greater safety. Suddenly the speeding boat made a fast turn, bounced on a wave, and sent Daws and the nonswimmer into the water. He held her head above water until the boat could circle back. Another swimmer dove into the water and helped support the struggling girl until she was hauled to safety aboard the boat. But as hands reached down to grab her rescuer's hand, Dawson Trotman sank out of sight. So died "the Navigator," giving his life to save another's—a powerful story of sacrifice that reminds us of the one who gave His life to save us all.

Because He loves us, Jesus died so that we might live.

Dawson Trotman's life story should also remind us that a faith commitment to Christ is eternal life assurance only if it continues in a personal daily relationship with Jesus as our friend and leader. Daws encouraged believers to study and memorize God's Word to inform their relationship with its author. Many encouragers were central to the Navigators' strategy for reaping a spiritual harvest. This has made them world leaders in winning souls and keeping them through one-to-one mentoring.

These lessons are designed to take you to the Bible for foundational Christian truths. What you will read and discuss with your Christian friend will help you live a life of conversation and cooperation with Jesus. He desires an ever-closer personal relationship with you, and He wants you to want the same.

You've said yes to the new way of life provided by God the Father through the death and resurrection of His Son, Jesus Christ. May God bless the rest of your life as you constantly experience this truth: "Anyone who belongs to Christ has become a new person. The old life is gone; a new life has begun! And all of this is a gift from God, who brought us back to himself through Christ" (2 Corinthians 5:17–18 NLT).

Part 1

God's plan has always been for Jesus to rescue you from hell to be His child.

A. Jesus is able to rescue you from going to hell (eternal punishment) because He is both God and man. The following tells who Jesus is and what He has done.

1. Jesus is God. As God, He had lived in heaven since before time began. Then He was born as a baby in Israel more than two thousand years ago, at just the right time according to God's plan.

2. Everything Jesus did on earth was good. As a man He lived to help others.

3. He lived exactly as God told Him to live; His perfect life shows us what God is like.

4. The Roman ruler over Israel, Pilate, executed Jesus at the request of Jewish leaders who were jealous of Jesus because of the crowds who followed Him. They hated Jesus because He exposed their sin.

5. When He died, Jesus took God's punishment for all the things you did wrong in God's eyes (called sin). Jesus himself never sinned, so He did not deserve to be punished. But He willingly suffered your punishment so you wouldn't have to (2 Corinthians 5:21).

6. God brought Jesus back to life, and then He returned to heaven to be eternal King. He rules now over every person who believes in Him and willingly obeys Him.

7. One day He will return to rule the whole world with love, justice, and total authority.

In the Bible, find the book called the Gospel of John, which tells about Jesus' life. You will need to read several sections of the book called John to complete this lesson.

B. Jesus came to rescue you from the punishment you deserved for rebelling against God.

1. The Bible tells us that every person is guilty of sin and deserves eternal punishment. You can read more about this in the book of John, chapter 3, verses 16–20 (John 3:16–20). Also read verse 36 of that same chapter of John (John 3:36).

    a. According to John 3:36, what will happen to every person who does not believe in Jesus Christ?

    b. What will such a nonbeliever not see or receive?

2. Before reading John 3:36, did you understand that sin—disobeying God—is that bad? What sinful things that you've done in the past still seem attractive in light of those eternal consequences?

3. When Jesus died, He was being punished for your crimes against God. According to John 3:16, why did He allow himself to be treated this way?

In the space below, write John 3:16, using your name instead of the terms *the world* and *whoever*.

4. After thinking about these truths, how do you feel…

    a. about your sins?

    b. toward Jesus, knowing what He did for you?

Now thank Him for what He has done for you. Say it to Him just as you would tell another person. Praying is as simple as that, and God always hears.

5. Did you…

    a. ask for forgiveness from Jesus, your sacrifice or sin payment (John 3:16)?

    b. believe in Jesus to be your friend forever—your Savior (John 1:12; 15:14)?

    c. commit to cooperate with Him daily as your leader and Lord (John 15:14)?

C. Jesus has rescued you to become God's child!

1. To all those who receive Jesus and believe on His name, what special right does Jesus give them? Read John 1:12.

2. How does it feel, deep down, to be God's own child?

3. You can now say, "God has put His own Spirit inside of _____ to stay forever." (Read John 14:17 and fill in the blank.)

4. As a child of God, you are now in God's family with new brothers and sisters. God wants your life to be part of theirs. Like a log in a fire that burns better in the presence of other logs, your new life with God will get stronger as you spend time in the presence of your new spiritual family. That's why you should become an active part of a church that believes that the Bible is God's message to humankind.

Jesus, fully God and fully human, was the only perfect sacrifice capable of paying the penalty for your sins. He died so that you might have a new life as a beloved child of God forever.

Part 2

God's plan for you is new life.

 Read John 3:1–8.

A. You have been "born again"—given a new nature by God's Spirit, who is living in you. Read about this in John 1:12–13 and 3:3–8.

1. Because of your spiritual birth, where will you one day be able to go that you would not otherwise be allowed to enter (John 3:3, 5)?

2. Spiritual birth brings spiritual life. Your new life makes it possible for you to obey your new King, something that was impossible before no matter how hard you tried to be good. Read John 8:34–36. Whose slave were you before Jesus set you free?

3. What is different about your life since you came to Jesus?

4. Explain what has happened inside of you—the difference Jesus has made. Would you call what this a miracle? Why or why not?

5. Explain to your Christian friend how you feel on the inside.

B. You are now a newborn spiritual baby who needs to grow and get to know God, your heavenly Father. Growing will always be connected to talking with God.

1. You were born again as a result of talking with God.

   a. Somehow you began to know that the story of Jesus as told in the Bible is true. That was God speaking to your heart.

   b. Then you talked to God when you asked Him to forgive you and to be your ruler. The result was your spiritual birth on _____ (date).

2. Your new position as God's child means you now have the privilege of personal contact with Him. A personal relationship grows with conversation—so you must continually listen to God and talk often with Him. See the Plan of Action, below, for instructions on how to do this.

God is now your heavenly Father, and you are His child. God's Spirit is living in you, so you are always in direct personal contact with God. Being close to God this way calls for ongoing conversation with Him.

Plan of Action

God's plan for you, His child, is to grow a personal relationship with you.

1. Conversation with God is best learned by setting aside a regular time and place each day to be alone and quiet with God. Start with fifteen to twenty minutes of time when you can talk with God and allow Him to speak to you. How does Matthew 6:6 tell us we should pray? Where and what time of day will you commit to doing this?

Where: _____   Time each day: _____

2. In your daily quiet time, do the following:

a. Ask God to help you receive His message for you through what you are about to read in His Word, the Bible (John 14:26). Just pay attention to what you can understand. This is "hearing" God talk to you through the Bible.

b. Begin reading the Gospel of John. Keep studying chapter 1 until you meet your friend for Session 2. Read this same chapter each day, and notice how you see something new every time.

c. Underline the parts that speak to you strongly. Put a question mark beside the parts you don't understand. Then use the Bible-study worksheet provided with this lesson, and write the things asked for on the worksheet. For your first day studying chapter 1 of John, write down everything the author says about Jesus; then write how those things apply to you. Just do your best as you get started on this new project. Your Christian friend will help you.

d. After your study time, it's time for you to talk. In your own words, talk to God about the important things you wrote about from the chapter you studied.

- Praise God for the things about Him you read and also for what He has done for you and for the ways He is helping you each day.
- Talk to God about whatever else comes to your mind.
- Be sure to thank Him for coming to live inside of you and for bringing you new eternal life.
- Tell God how wonderful it is for you to be forgiven and to now belong to Him through Jesus.
- Ask Him to help you with the problems you are struggling with.
- You can also ask Him to help other people with their problems, no matter what those problems are. Remember that God created the whole universe, so He has enough power to do anything. He can even heal sickness or injury, so don't hesitate to ask Him to do things that are impossible for man to do. With God, nothing is impossible!

Reminder: Things to Do This Week

1. Have quiet time each day, completing your Daily Journal (see Appendix A for a reproducible journal page) during this time, until you meet your friend for Session 2 on _____ (date).

2. Tell the people you usually see from day to day about the big and wonderful change Jesus has made in your life. Don't argue or try to answer every question

they may have—just tell them what has happened to you. You can use the material you've already covered in this course to help you explain it to them.

3. It's very important to make time to meet regularly with your Christian friend, who will help you understand what it means to be a Christian and pray for you every day. Also, attend the regular church meetings your friend encourages you to attend as a new Christian. Remember, a log needs other logs to burn well. Don't stay away from other Christians! You can find them at (write in church name, address, and meeting times):

Knowing God Is Always with You

Notes

Twelve-year-old Shayne didn't want to admit it even to himself, but he liked these new foster parents. His room wasn't as big as it had been at some of the other places, but this new couple asked him to call them Mom and Dad. No matter how badly Shayne acted, his foster father would always say, "Let's talk this through." And even when Shayne yelled and said unkind things, the man never lost his temper or raised his voice. He was firm and punished Shayne when he'd done wrong, but he always ended by telling the boy, "I love you, Son."

Shayne didn't dare believe it: he had been disappointed too many times before—sent back into the system when he became difficult or inconvenient. So he pushed hard and rebelled, trying to discover the limits of that love. But no matter how rough things got, he never did. "I'm not going away," Shayne's father often told him during his rages. "I'll always be here for you. Let me know when you want to talk."

In less than a year, the adoption was final. Shayne was a permanent member of his new family. But he knew he was really his father's son when he heard his calm response to a new foster sister's screams of frustration, "Let's talk this through."

You are now God's child, and you can always depend on Him to be with you.

You are now God's child, and you can always depend on Him to be with you. When you walk through life with God, you never have to worry that He won't want you or that you'll face anything that the two of you together can't handle.

"The Lord himself goes before you and will be with you; he will never leave you nor forsake you. Do not be afraid; do not be discouraged" (Deuteronomy 31:8). Can you hear Him whispering to your spirit: "I love you, Son; I love you, Daughter"?

As you spend time with your heavenly Father and talk with Him, you'll cultivate a close relationship and find yourself becoming more like Him. Today's lesson helps you understand how.

Part 1

Being God's child means God is always with you.

A. God loves you greatly, and His Spirit in you brings His love. Find the book of Romans in your Bible, and read chapter 5, verse 5 (Romans 5:5). What does this verse say that indicates God is generous with His love?

B. God is always in personal contact with you. Because He loves you, He is with you and is always giving you His personal attention. Here are four ways in which God works to be close to you:

1. Read John 1:29. God sent Jesus to remove the _____ from between you and God.

2. Read John 6:44–45. Since you have come to Jesus, how does this statement show that God wanted contact with you before you wanted contact with Him?

3. God is with you because His Spirit is in you. Read John 6:56. Jesus gives life to your spirit, so He compares himself to food and drink that gives life to your body.

   a. What do you have to do with food and drink before it can give life to your body?

   b. What did you do so that Jesus can give life to your spirit?

   c. The result, in Jesus' words, is:

   d. Read John 14:17. You and Jesus can be "in" each other by His _____ being in you.

4. God knows everything about you in every area of your life, no matter how small it may seem. How does Jesus explain it in Luke 12:6–7?

C. Because God loves you as His precious child, He wants you to feel His presence. He wants you to hear Him in your spirit when He talks to you, and He wants you to respond. Read Romans 8:15–16.

1. From Romans 8:16, what is God saying to you?

   Do you know in your spirit that He is saying this to you? (Circle one.)

   Yes   No   Not sure

2. From Romans 8:15, what does God want you to say back to Him?

3. From what you have read in the Bible, what do you think God feels toward you as His child?

4. How do you feel about God?

 You are God's child, learning to recognize the closeness of your heavenly Father.

Part 2

 # Being with God results in doing things with God.

A. Jesus' conduct came from His contact with God the Father.

1. Read Luke 6:12–13. What did Jesus do immediately before He made the important decision of calling His disciples? What role do you think giving God His full attention all night played in Jesus' decision? What lesson can you learn for your own life from Jesus' example?

2. Read John 4:31–34. What was even more satisfying to Jesus than having a meal when He was physically hungry? This would mean that Jesus' greatest appetite was to do what?

3. Read John 5:17–20, 30. How did Jesus know what He should do?

4. Read John 5:17; 14:10. How was Jesus able to do what He did?

B. God's commands tell you what He wants you to do with Him.

1. When human authorities give commands, they do not personally help others carry them out. God gives commands, but He always helps you to obey. What is one of God's commands you feel you especially need His help to obey?

2. Read again John 15:4–5. Does God ever want you to try to accomplish something alone, or with only other people's help?

3. God's works can only be done if you do them along with God. For each of these miracles, describe the person's part and God's part.

    a. John 2:1–11

    b. John 6:5–13

4. Like you, God enjoys doing things with someone He loves. That someone in this lesson is you. How do you feel about doing things with God?

5. Have you had an experience such as Jesus had, as described in John 4:31–34, when you did something God wanted you to do and it made you feel good and strong on the inside? Write about it on another piece of paper, or tell your Christian friend about it.

It so important as a new believer to remember that you are always in contact with God. He is paying attention to you all the time. How much attention should you be giving Him? Do you see why it is important to spend lots of time giving God your full attention by studying His Word, praying, and listening for His voice? The more we know God, the more we will love and want to please Him. And better yet, as we get to know Him, we learn to know what He wants and how to please Him. The more contact we have with our heavenly Father, the more our conduct will be His working through us.

 God wants constant contact with you. Always remember that He is with you. Talk to God often, and always listen and obey as you do everything with Him.

Plan of Action

God's desire for you is to listen to and know His voice.

1. Following are some guidelines for listening to God speak to you.

   a. You have already heard God speak to you through the Bible and in your heart, when He made you know that He wanted you to give your life to Him. You obeyed His voice. As you listen with the desire to obey, God will talk to you many times about many things.

   b. Not every spiritual voice is God's. Evil spirits can put thoughts in your mind that make you want to do selfish things. Any thought or desire that tells you to do something that disagrees with the Bible or with what you know about God's character is either from your own natural self or from an evil spirit. Tell such thoughts and desires to leave you, because Jesus is your King, and you only agree with Him and what He says to do. Read 1 John 4:1–3, and discuss with your friend how to distinguish God's voice from other voices that seek to influence you.

2. Sometimes when you read your Bible, words will seem to come alive, jump off the page, or burn in your heart. That is God's Spirit telling you something you especially need to know at that time. Give special attention to obeying what God has said to you this way after discussing with your friend what God is saying.

3. Have daily quiet time. (Read and take notes on chapters 2 through 6 in John before the next session.)

   a. Use the Daily Journal again with this session. Each day, read a chapter in John and write about the wonderful things you see in that chapter.

   b. Review and follow the guidelines for prayer from Session 1.

4. Start training yourself to speak with God often each day. He hears even your thoughts and will speak to you as you listen with your heart. You will learn to recognize certain thoughts in your mind and feelings in your heart as coming from God. God wants to speak often to you, so constantly listen for His voice. Make a practice of thanking God every hour for being with you and for all He has done for you.

5. Whenever you realize that you have acted or spoken apart from God, without giving Him your attention or without depending on Him, don't allow Satan to discourage you. Read 1 John 1:5–10. Without delay, do what verse 9 says, which is to:

What does God promise always to do in response?

6. It's important to tell others about your faith in Jesus. Read Matthew 10:16–20. When you tell someone about Jesus and how you are learning to know Him, you might notice that sometimes thoughts and words come into your mind and out of your mouth before you even know what you are saying. God helps His children say the right things when they talk to other people about Him.

Don't forget…He is always with you, giving you His full attention! Allow your contact with God to produce good conduct with God. Train yourself to constantly listen for God's voice to help you know what to do. Then depend on His help to do it. Most of the time it will be easy. Just think, "What would Jesus do?" If God wants you to do something less obvious, ask God, "Can You and I do this together?" He will tell you what to do, so listen. And always remember, He is always with you.

Reminder: Things to Do This Week

1. Continue studying and praying daily in your quiet time. Also, work through Session 3 by yourself before your next regular meeting with your Christian friend. In addition to discussing Session 3, tell him or her about times when you hear God speak to you, what you do in response, and what happens after that. And don't forget to keep attending regular church meetings at:

2. Write a Daily Journal entry for each chapter of the Bible you read each day. Keep moving forward in your study—details are best examined after you understand the main things. Your goal now is to see those main things. Keep in mind that God's Spirit is with you to help you understand as you put forth the effort to use the mind God gave you. Read John 14:26 and 16:13, and whenever you study, remember what Jesus promised.

Worshiping God, Loving God

The earliest known valentine is in the British Museum in London. It was sent by Charles, the Duke of Orleans, to his wife in 1415. It wasn't until the eighteenth century that sending valentines became a tradition. In their early forms, they were homemade, and the verses were composed by the sender specifically for the intended recipient.

God sent the greatest personal valentine message to all of us when "the Word became human and made his home among us" (John 1:14 NLT) "He existed in the beginning with God. God created everything through him.... The Word gave life to everything that was created, and his life brought life to everyone" (John 1:2–4 NLT). The greatest gift of love to mankind was when Jesus died on the cross for us. God gave His only Son to pay for our sins. When we accept Jesus Christ to be our personal Lord and Savior, it is an act of true worship—when our commitment comes from a heart filled with love for God in response to His love for us.

True worship always comes from a heart filled with love.

 Read Matthew 22:25–40.

Part 1

 True worship requires seeing God as He really is.

 Read John 4:23–24.

A. God is love, and He gives to you His true and pure love. Read Ephesians 2:4–10.

   1. According to 1 John 4:10, 19, who started loving first, God or mankind?

   2. According to Romans 5:6–8, did God love you because you were good?

B. God is spirit (John 4:24), so His love is spiritual.

   1. Read Romans 5:5. How and where does God pour out His love for you?

   2. God's love brings change, beginning on the inside.

     a. Your heart is changed by God's Spirit loving you (Ephesians 3:14–21).

     b. Read Romans 8:15–18. You know by the Spirit telling your spirit that you are God's _____.

   3. Read Romans 8:1–3, 12–14. Your natural self (what you are apart from God's influence in your life) is often called "flesh" in the Bible. It still wants to control what you do. But you don't have to obey its desires any longer. That control is now broken, as explained in verses 1–3. If you depend each moment on God's powerful Spirit in you, He will free you from obeying your old desires and give you spiritual strength to obey God instead. Read also Romans 6:6–13. Write what you learned from these passages in Romans.

C. You can only begin to see God as He really is after you receive Him and allow Him to love you.

   1. Read John 1:12–13. Who is given the right to become children of God?

   2. Read John 6:55–57. You are allowing Jesus to love you by receiving Him into your life, just as you allow food and drink to help you when you _____ and _____.

   3. You get a true view of God when you have a personal experience with Him. Read John 9:1–7, 35–38. Notice especially verses 37 and 38. The blind man began to understand Jesus' love for him after Jesus healed him. Likewise, you can see or understand God much better after you have allowed Him to show you His love for you in specific ways. What has God done for you that helps you understand Him better?

 When you see God as He truly is, you will worship Him in the proper way (John 4:24).

Part 2

 **True worship begins with expressing gratitude to God for His love that you have experienced.**

 Read Luke 17:11–19.

A. Gratitude is an inner recognition of the person who has shown love.

 1. Can a person receive benefits from God without being grateful to God for what He has done? (See Luke 17:17–18; Matthew 18:27–32.)

 2. Why do you think the nine lepers and the forgiven slave were ungrateful? What was different about the one leper who returned?

 3. Which are you more like, the grateful one or the ungrateful nine?

 4. Read Psalm 136, a song of praise and thanksgiving. In your quiet time, you may wish to write your own psalm thanking God for some of the wonderful things He has done for you.

B. Saying thank you gives honor to the one who gave, in recognition of the value of the benefit received.

 1. One leper responded with true gratitude to God. How does the leper's response in Luke 17:15–16 demonstrate true worship?

2. Read Philippians 4:6 and Ephesians 5:20. What does God desire from you in response to His love for you?

 It isn't enough to feel gratitude; we must express it.

Part 3

 True worship is giving your whole self to God, loving Him with every part of you. This is the only fitting response to the ways He already loves you.

 The First Commandment
Jesus said, "'Love the Lord your God with all your heart and with all your soul and with all your mind.' This is the first and greatest commandment" (Matthew 22:37–38). This is the essence of true worship. Let's look at these areas of love and worship one by one. You worship God by loving Him with…

A. All your heart.

   1. See first how valuable you are to God.

   2. Respond by making Him the greatest treasure of your heart.

B. All your soul.

   1. See first how deeply God feels for you and to what extent He gave Himself to serve you.

   2. Respond from your soul by feeling deeply for God and devoting your energies to serving Him.

C. All your mind.

   1. See how central you are in God's thoughts.

2. Respond by filling your daily thoughts with God and making Him the most important object of your study.

D. With all your heart…soul…mind.

Think about how valuable you are to God, how deeply He cares for you, and how central you are in His thoughts. Think also about the great price God paid for you, how long God plans to continue loving you, and how close to you He has made himself.

Since God loves you that much, the right kind of response is to love Him back with all of your heart, soul, and mind. The more you understand God's love for you, the more you will love Him so deeply and completely that you will put God above everything else in your life in importance to you and in your affection and thoughts. Worshiping love responds to God as the one who is most important in all of life—now and forever (1 John 2:15–17).

 We worship God when we love and serve Him with the sum total of all our parts—our will, our emotions, and our thoughts.

Part 4

 ### True worship is when your heart-love for God produces your actions.

A. With whom does a selfish heart cooperate in sinning (Ephesians 2:2–3)?

1. Read John 5:44; 8:23, 34, 38–47; 12:43; and 1 John 2:15–17. These verses show why most people do the things they do. What are some of the reasons?

2. Why does a selfish heart pretend to worship God? (Matthew 6:1–8)

3. Does God receive it?

B. God wants you to live from your heart, doing everything you do as part of your love for Him. This is worship in action.

1. Jesus set a perfect example. (See John 7:16–18; 8:26–29, 42, 50, 54–55.)

2. Read John 8:28–29. Even Jesus, the perfect Son of God, did nothing on His own but spoke just what the Father taught Him. What does this passage tell you, Jesus' disciple, about how your actions can be like His—all coming from the heart?

3. How do worshiping God, talking with God, and obeying God go together? (See John 8:29; 15:14–15.)

 Realize how important it is to God that you truly worship Him from your heart as you talk and walk with Him out of love for Him.

Plan of Action

 ## God's plan for you, His child, is that you love Him in return for loving you first.

1. God loved you first and is happy when you love Him in return. Loving God is a lot like loving a person. You give Him your attention, you talk with Him, you thank Him for what He does for you, and you show Him love in your actions. With God, this means willingly doing everything with Him, depending on His guidance and help. This is worship living!

2. Memorize the number-one command in Matthew 22:37, and make it your motto for the rest of your life. Pray daily to understand what to do to obey God, and ask Him to help you be able to do it.

3. Daily quiet time: Read John 7 to 11 before the next session. Remember to...

   a. Study. Write what you see in each chapter, using your Daily Journal.

   b. Pray. Continue to follow the guidelines in Session 1 and following:

   • Ask God to forgive you for the ways you have been disappointing Him by disobeying Him. Pray specifically about each time you have disappointed God.

- Thank Him for the promises you discover in His Word, saying them specifically. Tell God you are trusting Him to do what He promised, His way!
- Tell God about any struggles or problems you have, and ask Him to guide you and help you deal with them in His way.
- Ask God to heal you of any sickness or injury in your body. He may heal instantly or little by little. Sometimes God will tell you specifically what He will do if you pray and believe that He will do a certain thing. Sometimes you will pray and not know just how God will answer. You can always know that He does hear your prayer and that He will answer in the way that He chooses.
- Thank God again for coming into your life, for forgiving you, and for all the other things He has done for you recently.

Reminder: Things to Do This Week

1. Keep telling others about Jesus, encouraging them to receive Him as you did.

2. Be faithful in meeting with your friend and with your "family" in church.

3. Continue to regularly have your daily quiet time with God, using the Daily Journal system you started in Sessions 1 and 2.

4. Work through the material for Session 4 before your next meeting on:

Working with God

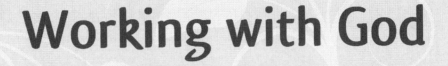

It has been said that following Christ means laying aside your right to choose whom to love. As Christians, we are commanded to love our neighbor as we love ourselves; to love the lovely and lovable as well as the unappealing and unlovable. That's a tall order, but we can be thankful that God does not leave us to accomplish this on our own.

"God is working in you, giving you the desire and the power to do what pleases him" (Philippians 2:13 NLT).

Did you catch that? God will work with us not only to give us the power to do what pleases Him and love others, but the desire also. You don't have to love those difficult people by yourself; but you do have to love them.

During the Revolutionary War, Peter Miller showed such love to a man who had sworn to be his enemy because of religious differences. Michael Widman spit in Miller's face whenever he came upon him, often tripped him, and was even known to punch him. But, full of the love of God, Miller responded with love and kindness.

One day Miller got word that Widman had been tried as a traitor to the Revolution and condemned to hang for his crimes. Miller walked seventy miles to plead for mercy from his old acquaintance, George Washington. General Washington was unmoved—until he learned that Widman was not Miller's friend but his worst enemy. The love of Christ that overflowed from Miller's life touched and changed George Washington's heart. It also changed Widman's. Washington pardoned him, and the former enemies walked home together, friends.

> ## Notes

God has called you to do wonderful things for Him— things too big for you to do on your own. But they're not too big for you and God to do together.

The love of God gave Peter Miller the desire and the power to show love even to someone our human nature would tell us not to love. When we follow Jesus, He helps us to lay aside our human nature and take up His godly nature.

Will you open your life for God to use you and accomplish His work? If so, get ready to love with a love that can only come from God. We'll learn how in this session.

 Read Philippians 2:13.

Part 1

 # God loves people and commands you to love people with His help.

A. God loves us through His Son, the Good Shepherd (John 10:1–18, 27–30).

1. Read John 10:1–18; 27–30, where Jesus calls himself the shepherd of the sheep or the Good Shepherd. Describe what the Good Shepherd does to show His love for us, His sheep.

2. After Peter had betrayed his love for Jesus and denied Him three times, Jesus gave Peter a second chance to know His love and show it to others. Read John 21:15–17. What did Jesus tell Peter to do?

3. Read 1 John 4:21. What do you hear Jesus saying to you? How is it similar to what He told Peter?

4. Read the top two commands Jesus identified in Matthew 22:36–39. Write the first, or greatest, command in your own words.

Write the second command in your own words.

Read its companion verses in John 13:34 and 1 John 4:21.

How can you love as God does? (See John 13:34; 1 John 3:16; 5:2.)

B. God's love for you fills you with love that overflows to other people (1 John 4:7–21).

   1. All love begins and flows from God (1 John 4:9–10, 16, 19). You must obey the first command by loving God to keep on receiving God's love. According to John 14:20–23, what is the second component besides love?

   2. You can give to others from the love you have received from God, which is obeying the second command. Copy the phrases in 1 John 4:7–12 that tell about loving others out of the love you receive from God

        Read 2 Corinthians 1:3–4, which gives a similar message about how we can share with others what God gives to us.

   3. When you love your other spiritual family members this way, what does it prove? (See John 13:35 and 1 John 4:7.)

        Notice that Jesus said "*are* my disciples," not *were*. This kind of love proves that you are now connected to Jesus as His disciple. You can only love others with Jesus' kind of love if you are receiving that love yourself from Jesus through your connection with Him as His disciple. (See 1 John 3:9–18; 4:7, 12.)

   4. How important is it for God's love to be flowing through you to others? (See 1 John 3:10, 14–15; Matthew 5:43–48.)

   5. How can you know the right way to love your neighbor, as described in the second command (Matthew 22:39)?

   6. The best way of loving yourself is to allow God to love you as you trust and obey Him. The best way of loving your neighbors as yourself is to help them receive God's _____ by…

     a. Being a channel of God's loving kindness to them.

     b. Helping them know God personally so they can receive His love directly as they trust and obey Him.

 God pours His love into you so His love can overflow to others.

Part 2

Love responds to particular needs.

A. People's needs are different and require different actions on our part to meet them. Read about the neighbor in Luke 10:29–37.

   1. List all the acts of love and mercy that are shown in the story.

   2. Review the story of the unforgiving servant in Matthew 18:27-33. What sort of mercy was needed in Matthew 18:27 and 33?

   3. Jesus came because His Father loved the world so much (John 3:16). Love cares about needs. What was the greatest need Jesus came to meet? (See John 11:25–26, 40–45; 12:44–50.)

 Stay calm. Relax. Sharing your story about what Jesus has done for you doesn't have to be scary. People can and will argue with you about what you believe, but they can't argue about what has happened to you.

B. Being a witness is responding to mankind's greatest need.

   1. When you tell your family and friends about how Jesus has changed your life, you are being a _____ about Jesus to them.

      a. Remember, you are loving your neighbors—people near you—as yourself by helping them know how to receive God's love.

      b. When you witness, tell your story peacefully, with faith that the _____ will do His part, which is to _____ _____. (See John 16:7–8.)

   2. What does 1 Peter 3:15 tell you to always be ready to do?

   3. To help you get prepared to do this, take a blank sheet of paper. Write on one side the story of how you put your faith in Jesus. Work on it until it is

clear and short. You can always add details from memory when talking, if time allows.

4. Some people are not interested in hearing about Jesus, or they will be angry or scornful toward you when you speak of Jesus. Join many Christians around the world in praying for genuine love for people whether they receive or reject you. Pray also for boldness to speak the simple message of Christ with gentleness and respect and without being restrained by fear. (Read more about this in Matthew 5:43–48 and Acts 4.)

 Think of God's heartbeat as saying, "Peo-ple/peo-ple/peo-ple" (say it aloud). Ask God to give you a heart for people full of His love and His power to show it.

Plan of Action

God's plan for you, His child, is for you to love and to share His love with others.

1. Start a list of ways to obey the top two commands (Matthew 22:37, 39). Keep the list close by as a reminder and a place to make additions as you think of them. Remember, whatever God commands you to do, He helps you to do. The key is to ask for His help and keep asking (Matthew 7:7–8). Then act in faith that He will help you do it.

2. Daily quiet time: Study John chapters 12 through 16 before the next session.

   a. Study each chapter and write what you see, using the Daily Journal system.

   b. Continue to pray as guided previously and in whatever ways brought to mind by the notes from your study of John. Ask God to guide you and give you strength and to help you overflow with His love. Also, ask Him to lead you to people whose hearts He is already preparing and to help you say whatever He wants you to say in love.

3. Discuss with your discipling friend what you are learning from the book of John. Share how God has helped you obey as well as how you have failed to obey. He or she will celebrate with you God's pleasure in your victories and God's forgiveness for your defeats (remember 1 John 1:9). Your friend will also guide you, encourage you, and pray that God will help you to cooperate with God to produce the right attitudes and actions in your day-to-day living.

Your Spiritual Birth Announcement

The young, eager camp counselors sat around the campfire during their orientation seminar just before the start of youth camp. They went around the circle giving their names, ages, and a brief testimony. When they got to a curly-haired blond man whose thick glasses seemed to intensify the passion in his eyes, he boldly proclaimed: "My name is Larry Koski, and I'm 4 years, 3 months, and 14 days old. That was when Larry Kosinski died, Jesus took my sin away, and I was born again as Larry Koski. I followed the Lord in water baptism and have followed Him in fellowship and service for 4 years, 3 months, and 14 days."

That's a pretty good illustration of water baptism. It's like a funeral service and a birthday party rolled into one. The funeral part is saying good-bye to the old, selfish you that has died with Christ. The birthday celebration is the joyful recognition of the new you—raised up to new life after being born of God into His family.

The new believer generally proclaims in simple words that he or she now belongs to Jesus. This adds verbal testimony to the message of their public act of water baptism in the name of Jesus Christ.

Baptism is usually conducted in a church building, with other believers present as representatives of the family of God as it welcomes a new brother or sister. Other public venues are common, such as swimming pools, rivers, lakes, or seashores—often with others present as well. Most churches totally immerse the baptismal candidate in water.

More important than the mode of baptism, however, is that it follows and testifies to one's personal decision to follow Jesus Christ.

When you are baptized in water, you are obeying God and being a witness.

Mike
Mike Wallace.
pray for race—
marathon

Deb here friend
Colean - making
chicken dumplins

Virginia - Brian
+ Kathy friend

Matt + family - Mike
where friends

Wanda

Part 1

Water baptism is a public announcement of your new faith in Jesus.

A. Water baptism should always follow a decision to place one's faith in God through Jesus.

1. In Matthew 28:19, whom does Jesus say to baptize?

2. In Mark 16:16, whom does Jesus say qualifies for water baptism?

3. Who was baptized in the early church (Acts 2:38, 41; 8:12)?

B. Being baptized shows our faith in Jesus as our Savior and our new leader. Trust in a leader is demonstrated by following.

1. In Matthew 28:18–20, Jesus gives instructions regarding baptism. These instructions are (circle one) suggestions/commands.

2. When you obey Jesus, you are showing your _____ for Him (John 14:15).

3. The early Christians obeyed this command. Read about them in Acts 2:38, 41; 8:12; 9:18; 10:48; 16:33; 18:8. Will you join them in obeying this command? When?

 By being baptized in water, you are announcing your faith in Jesus and showing your love for Him by obeying His command.

Part 2

Water baptism is an illustration of conversion.

Read Romans 6:1–7.

A. Water baptism helps us visualize the spiritual work of forgiveness. Acts 22:16 describes baptism as washing your sins away. It's like you are going under water sinful and dirty and coming up forgiven and clean.

    1. The Bible word for sin that has been paid for is *justification* (being justified: Romans 5:1). The process of justification is described in Romans 6:3–7.

        a. God sees you as if _____ death was your own, because Jesus' death pays in full the debt for your sins (Romans 6:5).

        b. Because the penalty demanded by God's law has been paid by Jesus, you are no longer _____, but under grace (Romans 6:14).

        c. With your debt now paid, you are no longer condemned by God's law (Romans 8:1–2). How does that make you feel?

    2. Now that you are no longer condemned by sin to eternal death, you have also been set free from sin's control of your conduct. Jesus has broken the power of sin in your life.

        a. Romans 6:6–7 says: "Our old self was crucified with him so that the body of sin might be done away with [or be rendered powerless—the actual meaning of the original language], that we should no longer be _____ to sin—because anyone who has died has been _____ from sin."

        b. Romans 6:12 says: "Do not let sin _____ in your mortal body." When sin reigns, you _____ its evil desires. (See also Romans 6:14.)

        c. The things in your own life that used to control you, but don't anymore, include:

B. According to Romans 6:4, you are raised with Jesus to _____. That means going under water as if buried—then being raised up as if resurrected with new life.

    1. You are free from sin and free to _____ with Jesus (Romans 6:8).

    2. Because you are now joined with Jesus, you are free to behave in a new and better way (Romans 6:4–22).

        a. New behavior is now possible for you (John 14:8–18; 15:4–17).

   b. New behavior is now necessary for you (John 15:1–6).

   c. Your new behavior is evidence of a relationship with the Father, as it was for Jesus (John 14:5–11).

3. You have been raised with Jesus to eternal life (Romans 6:5, 9, 22–23).

   a. What will happen to your body when it is raised from death (1 Corinthians 15:3–8, 35–57)?

   b. Where will you live for eternity (John 12:25–26; 14:1–3)?

> By being baptized in water, you are enacting a drama that says you have "died to sin"—sin no longer condemns you or controls you—and you have been "raised up" to live a new life of following Jesus.

Plan of Action

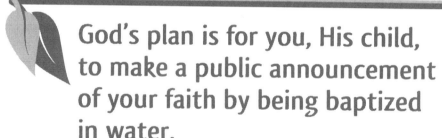

God's plan is for you, His child, to make a public announcement of your faith by being baptized in water.

1. The visible action of your being baptized is a statement in itself of your faith in Christ. You can make an additional strong statement when you allow God to use you to speak a few sincere words into the hearts of nonbelievers present. Your words will also bring rejoicing to your spiritual family who are welcoming you into God's kingdom. Ask God to put in your mind what He wants you to say to be a witness for Him. Don't worry about it—just pray seriously and believe that God's Spirit will give you the right words. Trust Him—and open your mouth.

2. Daily quiet time: Work through John 17 through 21 before your next session.

   a. Study each chapter, using the Daily Journal system. Complete one of these studies for each chapter in John, and save them in a notebook or folder.

b. Continue to pray as guided in Sessions 1–3 and as prompted by your studies. Make a special point today of asking God to make your water baptism a birth announcement that God will use to speak to the hearts of your unbelieving family and friends—and also that your daily behavior would continuously highlight the change Jesus can bring to a person's life. Use Matthew 5:16 as a guide for your praying.

 ## Reminder: Things to Do This Week

1. Ask your Christian friend about making arrangements to be baptized in water. Or go ahead and talk with the pastor of the church you attend to arrange for your spiritual birth announcement.

2. In preparation for your Christ-honoring baptism, pray about and plan your testimony—as explained in points 1 and 2 of this session's Plan of Action.

3. Continue your quiet time each day, and work through Session 6 before your next meeting with your friend, which will be on:

For Serious Seekers
Preview Evangelism
The "Four Before" Plan

Situations

Many Americans have heard some presentation of the good news with an appeal to receive Christ. They may feel the Holy Spirit drawing them, but they hold back because they have no practical idea of what life would be like if they committed themselves to Jesus. They resist because they don't know what they would be getting into.

Many other Americans have somewhere, at sometime, prayed a salvation prayer but failed to continue in the faith. They want to be Christians, but they need more understanding of how to live the Christian life successfully so they will not make the same mistakes as they did before. They are afraid they will fail a second time.

A Solution: Preview Evangelism—the "Four Before" Plan

1. Use Sessions 1 through 4 as a discussion guide, giving the next session to the nonbeliever to take home after each meeting. If the person would like to do the sessions *before* meeting with you, provide them accordingly.

2. After discussing Session 4, review the truths covered. Ask your friend to indicate whether he or she is ready to make a decision. If the decision is positive, proceed with the salvation prayer as taught in the Plan of Action in Session 14.

3. With rejoicing, arrange to continue meeting, now with you as the discipling friend and your new brother or sister as the new believer, to continue with Sessions 5 through 15.

Knowing God as Your Father

A daughter wrote the following message to her father:

Dad, I have always been so proud and grateful that you are my father. It makes me feel good to see how much so many people love and respect you. The older I get, and the more people I meet who have had such terrible (and yet "normal" for these days) fathers, it makes me all the more grateful for the wonderful father I have. I appreciate so much that I never had to fight the TV or sports for your attention. And I feel so blessed that you are a godly father who is always praying for our family and caring about all of us.

You have made it a natural and good thing for us kids to be able to see God as our heavenly Father, which is hard for many people. And you've always done a great job of giving us the direction and attention we need.

I'm also grateful that you are such a great husband to Mom, and although she assures me you aren't perfect, you certainly set the bar high.

I hope your grandson will appreciate your example as much as I have and that he will strive to be a godly husband and father like you one day.

I love you.

In Matthew 6:9–13 Jesus opens His model prayer with, "Our Father in heaven…." It seems it is God's plan for children to get an early understanding of what He is like from their relationship with their natural father. Tragically, in modern times many fathers have fallen short of reflecting God's character in the ways they relate to their children. This lack on the part of human fathers makes it difficult for many new believers to see God as their heavenly Father in a positive way. But God will go the extra mile to reveal himself as the Father He is to those who struggle in this way—even to those who have never known their earthly father. Psalm 68:5 tells us God is "a father to the fatherless."

Don't assume that God is just like your earthly father. If your father has reflected God's nature, be thankful. If you feel there has been a breakdown in some ways, let God show you the kind of father He really is.

Part 1

God wants you to see Him as your Father in heaven when you pray.

A. True love and worship require a clear view of God (John 4:22–24).

1. God wants you to see Him and relate to Him as He is / as you think He ought to be. (Underline one.)

2. God sees you and relates to you as you are / as you want Him to see you. (Underline one.)

3. How is your Father in heaven like and unlike your earthly father? Keep this question in mind as you study this session. Write your answer here after you have completed the session.

 Jesus gives you a guide for praying and living. It is commonly called the Lord's Prayer.

B. As your Father, God has adopted you as His beloved, eternal child.

1. How do you feel, knowing that the one true and living God, the creator of the whole universe, is actually your own Father?

2. Read Romans 8:14–18. Why do you think God would want you to call Him Father?

3. How is God's father's heart shown in Matthew 10:29–31?

4. The prayer Jesus taught in Matthew 6:9–13 shows you that God, your Father, already wants to do things for you, His child. What are those things?

5. According to Matthew 7:7–11, what is one thing you must do to receive from God?

6. What plans does God have for your future (Ephesians 2:6–7)?

C. How are you responding to your Father in heaven?

1. Have you experienced the feelings described in Romans 8:15–16 and Hebrews 4:15–16? Explain.

2. Read the promise in Romans 8:28. Everyone has been tempted at times to think that God has failed him or her in some way. Have you? Explain.

3. Jesus himself endured the greatest test of faith when He died for your sins. Feel His struggle, faith, and victory as recorded in John 16:32 and Mark 15:34.

 Your Father in heaven is patient with your faith struggles as your trust in Him as your loving, heavenly Father grows. Knowing this will add much meaning to those wonderful verses in Hebrews 2:14–18; 4:14–16. Be quick to pray the prayer in Mark 9:24.

Part 2

Your Father in heaven wants you to know His loving authority.

 Read Matthew 6:9–10, 13.

A. What words here tell of God's authority?

B. How much authority does God have, and why does He have so much? Think carefully about the passage above as well as about 1 Timothy 6:13–16 before writing your answer.

C. What feelings do you have when you recognize that your Father in heaven has this much power and authority? (Notice the feelings described in Matthew 10:28–42; Hebrews 2:14–18; 4:1–2,11–16.)

 God has, along with His great love for us, ultimate authority over the universe and all in it. As such, He is worthy of our respect and reverence.

Part 3

 # Your Father/King wants you to see His holy nature.

Read Matthew 6:9.

A. Real love desires real understanding. God wants you to understand His holiness, and He wants you to help others to see Him as holy. Think carefully about the following to better understand why God wants you to pray that His name would be considered hallowed, or holy.

1. Holy means "set apart as sacred and pure."

2. *Name* refers to the reputation of the one who bears that name—the kind of person most people think that person is.

3. When you pray the phrase, "hallowed [holy] be your name," you are asking God to help you and other people to see God as holy and to better understand His holiness.

B. Study Revelation 4:1–11, and write the key words and phrases that describe the holiness of God in heaven.

 Prayer should usually begin with looking at God. Be careful to allow God to present the true picture of himself through His written Word and through His Spirit.

Plan of Action

God's plan for you, His child, is that you should remain connected to Him as your heavenly Father.

1. Isn't it amazing that you can come directly and personally to the King who is above every king on earth or in the spirit world and be loved and cared for directly and personally by this great King who is, in fact, your own Father forever? You can know God himself—if that is your greatest desire in life and if you stay focused on Him. Sessions 6 through 10 will take you section by section through the Lord's Prayer—a model prayer that Jesus gave to help you in the process of knowing God. Go ahead and start using the whole prayer as a guide for your praying. Before you finish these sessions, God will show you things as you pray this prayer. Ask God to really help you tune in to this study of the Lord's Prayer and to what He wants you to discover as you pray.

2. The Lord's Prayer begins with worship. See God as He is revealed in this prayer, and honor Him by praying in response to what you see.

    a. Tell Him what you see.

    b. Praise Him for who and what He is and for what He has done.

    c. Thank Him for what He has done for you.

    d. Tell Him you are honored to be able to tell others about Him.

    Here is an example of how to talk with God:

    "God, I thank You that You are not an angry and cruel tyrant who makes me shake with fear. You are my Father in heaven. You are holy, and I am sinful, but I can freely come to You because Your Son Jesus paid the penalty for my sins. I love You, Father, and I want to be a child who pleases You with my love. Help me to eagerly tell others about You so they can worship You as holy and know Your great love."

Now, you pray in your own words. God is not interested in beautiful words. Rather, He loves prayers that are simple and from your heart.

3. The following the L-O-R-D outline below is a way of remembering the sections you have studied:

   a. **L**ook at God (Matthew 6:9, 13). Worship Him at the beginning and end of your prayer.

   b. **O**rder your day His way (verse 10).

   c. **R**equest your daily supplies (verses 11–12).

   d. **D**epend on Him all day (verse 13).

Reminder: Things to Do This Week

1. Daily quiet time: Congratulations on finishing John! Now begin a study on Matthew 6:1–15, which is Jesus' teaching on prayer.

2. Continue to pray as instructed in Sessions 1 through 3, using the Lord's Prayer as an added guide.

3. Work through Session 7 before you meet your friend again on:

PRAY Guide
How to Pray for One Lost Person

A simple format to guide your praying for individual lost persons can be remembered with the word PRAY:

P **Problems** my friend is having because Jesus is not in control of his or her life:

R Ways my friend is **refusing** to trust Jesus to guide and provide for him or her:

A Things I am **asking** God to do to help my friend come to Jesus:

Y **Yes**, I will obey God in the following ways to help my friend come to Jesus:

You are a Citizen of Heaven

It seemed that everything had fallen apart. Jesus' statements that the kingdom of heaven was at hand seemed like wishful thinking. The disciples had anticipated having lead roles in an imminent government with Jesus as King. They even competed with each other for position. Then, after getting their hopes up, it seemed that Jesus had developed a death wish, for He openly antagonized the Jewish leadership until they engineered his death at the hands of the hated Romans. How can you have a kingdom without a king? It was over.

Then the unimaginable happened. Jesus was unmistakably alive again! Now with an indestructible king, they imagined that things would go quite well. They asked, "Lord, has the time come for you to free Israel and restore our kingdom?" (Acts 1:6 NLT). Jesus' reply redirected their thinking. They were believing in the right person, but they had the wrong plan. Jesus had not launched a forced-rule kingdom but an invisible, spiritual kingdom. His kingdom is not defined by a set of rules for good behavior but rather by a person's relationship with and obedience to the King himself. God's kingdom is present wherever His will is being done on earth, reflecting the worshipful obedience He receives in heaven.

God wants children who want to obey Him and who want others to obey Him.

For Peter to take a lead role in Christ's ongoing work on earth, Jesus had to make sure Peter understood that work. Their seaside breakfast conversation (John 21) focused on Peter's personal relationship with Jesus. Three times Jesus asked, "Peter, do you love me?" Each time Peter affirmed his love, Jesus gave him a command. He ended the conversation by twice repeating to Peter: "Follow me" (John 21:19, 22). Jesus' command reiterates a theme in John's gospel as Jesus several times told His followers that if they loved Him, they would keep His commandments (John 14:15, 21, 23). True love for Jesus is evident not only by feelings of love but also by obedience. God's kingdom comes wherever

believers truly follow Him in obedience to His will—both written and spoken by His Spirit.

Note: This principle is unique to the Christian faith. For example, the story is told that when Buddha was dying, his followers asked how they could best remember him. He told them that remembering him was not important: it was his teaching they should remember. But in Christianity, Jesus Christ is central. While His teaching is of great importance, without the ongoing presence of the resurrected Christ and the personal relationship that He offers to share with us, Christianity is dead and we are deluded and condemned. (The apostle Paul makes a strong case for this truth in 1 Corinthians 15.)

Jesus has called you not to a religion but to a relationship with Him. This relationship gives you a citizenship in His kingdom, where you aren't obeying impersonal laws but a personal King.

Part 1

God has a kingdom on earth now.

Read Matthew 6:10, 13.

A. God's kingdom is where people obey the King because they love and trust Him. ("Your will be done.")

1. Jesus said that if you _____ Him, you will do what He says (John 14:15).

2. Obedience is also an act of _____, as stated in Romans 1:5.

 a. Obedience shows faith and trust in the authority and wisdom of the one giving the command (Romans 1:3–4).

 b. Obedience shows faith and trust that the one we're obeying will care for us (Matthew 6:11–13, 33).

B. God's kingdom comes (increases) when obedience increases.

1. When you obey God more, His kingdom comes more through your actions.

2. When more people become Christians, God's kingdom grows. God's kingdom grew on your spiritual birthday, which was on _____.

3. When you pray for and help others come to Jesus—or help them to obey Him more—you are helping God's kingdom come. Describe something you did recently that helped God's kingdom come a little more in this way.

We have a role to play in advancing God's kingdom on the earth now.

Part 2

Obeying God includes obeying His authorities on earth.

  Read Romans 13:1–7.

A. What are God's reasons for having earthly rulers (Romans 13:4)?

1. How does God want the following people in authority to act toward the people under their authority?

   a. Governments (Romans 13:3–4)

   b. Job supervisors/employers (Colossians 4:1)

   c. Church leaders (Hebrews 13:17)

   d. Parents (Ephesians 6:4)

   e. Husbands (Ephesians 5:25–29)

2. _____ holds earthly rulers accountable for how they act toward the people under their authority (Romans 13:6; Ephesians 6:9; Hebrews 13:17).

B. God has planned for us to show different kinds of obedience to different authorities (Romans 13:7–8).

1. Children are to _____ their parents (Ephesians 6:1–2).

2. Wives are to _____ to and _____ their husbands (Ephesians 5:22–24, 33).

3. According to 1 Thessalonians 5:12–13 and Hebrews 13:7, 17–19, how should church members relate to church leaders?

4. How should employees act toward their bosses (Ephesians 6:5–7)?

5. How should citizens treat civil authorities (Romans 13:1–7; 1 Timothy 2:1–2)?

C. God blesses those who obey Him by obeying earthly authorities.

1. Write the promises of Ephesians 6:1–8.

2. If you trust God and keep an obedient spirit, God will overrule the effects of mistreatment or poor leadership that may come to you through earthly authorities. Be encouraged by reading Romans 8:28 several times.

 Submission—obedience to those in authority—does not always mean we must keep silent. Rather, submission is willing cooperation with those in authority.

3. In Romans 8:28, to whom does God make the promise of all things working together for good? Are you included in this group?

4. What difficulty with authority are you struggling with now? Pray with Romans 8:28 in mind. What things in your present situation are difficult to believe that God will work together for your good?

 As you willingly do what God wants you to do, it frees God's Spirit to do a work in the person in authority— even if that person is a nonbeliever. That's part of God's working things together for good.

5. Can you think of any good that God may be wanting to do in your life—to teach you, change you, or to change your circumstances—by allowing this situation in your life? Are you trusting God and obeying Him?

6. What changes do you think God wants you to make in the way you respond to that difficult authority?

7. According to Acts 4:18–20, what should you do when human authorities demand direct disobedience to God?

 Living with the coming of God's kingdom always in your thoughts and prayers will bring glory to God and good to you. Consider the results of rebellion since Genesis 3:1–24. Live now as a citizen of God's future kingdom that will last for eternity.

Plan of Action

God's plan for you, His child, is that you should be willingly obedient.

1. The Lord's Prayer begins with worship (look at God) and continues with surrender to the will of the King (order your day His way). Use Matthew 6:10 as a guide for the second stage of your praying according to this model prayer. Here is an example:

"Lord, I want Your kingdom to come to the way I live my life today. Help me to keep paying attention to You so You can direct me and give me power to do Your will throughout this day. I especially need help with… [name any situation in which you expect to be tested that day]. May Your will be done in others' lives [name them] also." (Then pray for God's will in these people's lives—and be specific.)

2. Whose authority is difficult for you to willingly obey? Ask God to fill your heart with love for this person (remember Matthew 5:43–48) and to give you an attitude of willing obedience. (Go ahead and act with proper

obedience, as if you have the attitude of willing obedience. You will be amazed to find that the right feelings and attitudes come to you from the Lord after you take the right actions. Remember: right feelings will follow right actions.) As you, by the power of the Spirit, submit willingly to the authority as if to God, your conduct is providing God with another channel through which He can work in the life of that person. Your submission also gives God more room to work in your own life. God blesses the person who rightly obeys.

3. Daily quiet time: Continue your study of all or part of Matthew 6:1–15. Continue to pray as instructed in Sessions 1 through 3 and as prompted by your quiet time studies in Matthew 6.

Reminder: Things to Do This Week

1. Continue having your quiet time each day and completing your Daily Journal. Work through Session 8 before your next meeting on:

2. Do whatever God puts in your heart from your study and prayer.

Your Daily Supply of Food

A mother shared the following testimony:

When our son Joshua was born with major heart defects, my husband and I committed him to God, confident that God loved him more than we did. After five heart surgeries, many hospital stays, and many medications, Joshua finally required open-heart surgery at age fifteen. His heart transplant at age seventeen was followed by near-fatal complications, long hospitalizations, and another serious surgery. Then he was diagnosed with non-Hodgkin's lymphoma in both lungs—a side effect of the necessary immuno-suppression medication. God brought him and us through all these crises.

Doctors had told us that we were in for a lifetime of expenses and warned us never to drop or be late with insurance-premium payments. Medical expenses accumulated against the million-dollar cap on Joshua's Blue Cross and Blue Shield insurance policy. Now we were approaching the policy's payout limit, and we knew no other company would insure him. If we lost his insurance, we would surely lose our home. Everything we earned after our tithe and living expenses went into insurance premiums and medical expenses.

One day I calculated the bills, and they came to $999,700. We were just a few hundred dollars from having no insurance for Joshua. I cried to the Lord, as I had so many times. I felt helpless surrounded by all the bills but prayed that God would help us.

That afternoon the phone rang. The woman on the other end said, "I'm calling regarding your son Joshua's insurance policy." My heart pounded, wondering if this might be the dreaded call. She said: "Blue Cross and Blue Shield's name has changed to Alliance Blue Cross and Blue Shield. The law says that if one word in a company's name changes, every policyholder's payout amount must be rolled back to zero." One little word—Alliance—had just given Joshua another million-dollar cap on his insurance policy.

God will provide for you as you worship, obey, and ask Him to "give us this day our daily bread."

I was numb, I cried, and I praised the Lord. I knew that He had been in control all the time. I have never ceased to testify to God's intervention and provision. We truly believe that if we are faithful to tithe to the Lord with what is already His, we can trust Him to meet our needs.

 Read Matthew 6:11.

Part 1

 ## God is the source of provision for all of your physical needs.

 Read Psalm 23:1.

A. God is able to provide.

1. According to Psalm 24:1, how much does God own? Whose property are you and your things (Psalm 24:1; 1 Corinthians 6:20)?

2. Read Psalm 104. What does the writer say that shows God is able to provide for you out of what He has?

3. Read Matthew 6:25–30 and circle the phrase that makes this sentence true: God's resource is sometimes not enough / just enough / always more than enough to meet my need. (Think of the implication of the father's statement about his possessions in Jesus' story in Luke 15:31.)

B. God wants to provide for your physical needs (Matthew 6:25–34).

1. God always knows your need for food and clothing (Matthew 4:4; 6:11).

a. When does He know what you need (Matthew 6:8)?

b. Think again about what Jesus says in Matthew 6:8, 26, 32. How much do you think He knows about what you need? (See also Matthew 10:29–30.)

2. Does God promise to supply what you need or what you want (Matthew 6:19–21)?

3. When does He promise to supply: when you want to have it, or when you need it (Hebrews 4:16)?

C. You and God are partners in your life. Do your part, and you can be sure God will do His part to provide for you.

1. God wants you to _____ Him to supply what you need (Matthew 6:11; 7:7–11). Why do you think He wants you to do this?

2. What does God want you to pursue first, something that is far more important than having material things? See what Jesus says in Matthew 6:32–33.

   a. Who in this world seeks material things first (Matthew 6:32)?

   b. Why is it not necessary for you to make pursuing material things your first priority?

   c. If you put obeying God above meeting your own physical needs, should you worry that you might not have what you need? Why or why not?

 Jesus commands you not to worry about your physical needs. If you pursue first what is most important to God, He has promised to provide the essentials for your physical needs.

Part 2

Giving tithes and offerings is God's way for you to use your money to seek His kingdom first.

A. Money by itself is not valuable—we give money in exchange for what is of real value to us. What you give money for shows what is important to you.

1. Read Acts 20:33–35. Jesus said: "It is more blessed to _____ than to _____." See also Ephesians 4:28. Why is showing kindness—sharing with those in need—so important for a Christian?

2. Can your money help God's kingdom come? How?

3. Are you willing to seek God's kingdom first in the way you spend money? In Matthew 6:33, what does God promise if you do?

B. The tithe (literally a tenth: a person who tithes gives to God one tenth of his gain in money, property, crops, or animals) was an amount used in the ancient world for taxation or for honoring someone in a higher position.

1. Abraham gave a tenth of his spoils of war to honor Melchizedek (Genesis 14:16–20).

2. Jacob promised to give God a tithe if God would provide for him materially and physically (Genesis 28:10–22).

3. God commanded the nation of Israel to pay Him a tithe of all kinds of material gain (Leviticus 27:30–32). They were to give their tithe to the priests as if they were giving it to God. God instructed that some of it should be used to support the priests as well as widows, orphans, and strangers. Much of the tithe collected was used for sacrifices to God.

4. God promised His people abundant blessing if they would honor Him with their tithes by giving the full amount as worship from the heart (Malachi 1:6; 3:7–12).

   a. Sincere tithers in Old Testament times were honoring God. To withhold the tithe was to rob God of honor due Him (Malachi 1:6; 3:7–12).

   • They were honoring God as creator, supreme ruler, and owner of all the earth. This means God also owned all of "their" possessions and material gain (Psalm 24:1).

   • They were honoring God as the provider for all their physical needs (Psalm 23:1–2).

    b. Tithers gained from God's hand by giving to Him, much like a farmer gains from God's increase from grain he puts in His earth (Malachi 3:10–11).

C. Offerings are voluntary gifts of goods or money to meet others' physical or spiritual needs. Gifts can be given directly to needy recipients or indirectly, through church leaders or agencies that will pass it on to those in need. This was a common demonstration of love that was commanded and practiced in the New Testament church. Both the command and the practice apply to us today as well.

    1. The New Testament practice of giving is described in the following passages. Summarize in your own words what each passage says.

        a. Acts 2:44–45; 4:34–35; 20:33–35

        b. 2 Corinthians 9:1–6, 11–12

        c. Philippians 4:14–18

    2. Such giving was also commanded and expected in the New Testament. Summarize in your own words the following passages.

        a. 2 Corinthians 9:6–15

        b. Galatians 6:6—giving to support church leaders and missionaries (See also Philippians 4:10–18.)

        c. Ephesians 4:28

        d. James 2:14–17

    3. How is this session affecting how you see your finances?

D. God still blesses those who honor Him with material resources.

    1. The best guideline for honoring God with your income is the guideline from the Old Testament of giving one tenth as a regular act of worship each

time you receive income. As an act of worship, the tenth should be given first, to show God that you want to honor Him as the first priority of your (His, actually) income. This also demonstrates faith that He will supply your needs as you give first to Him. Giving to the local church where you are under spiritual supervision and where you are regularly taught God's Word (Galatians 6:6) is similar to the Old Testament practice of giving to support the local priests as well as needy widows and other benevolence needs (Malachi 3:10).

2. God provides for Christians who give.

    a. Paul told the Philippian church that sent money for his needs: "My God will _____ all your _____" (Philippians 4:19).

    b. In 2 Corinthians 9:5–15, read Paul's words to the church that had promised a gift for struggling fellow Christians in Jerusalem. Write in your own words the main points Paul was making.

3. God also gives the giver more so she or he may continue giving to others (2 Corinthians 9:8–11).

4. According to 2 Corinthians 9:7, what kind of giver does God love?

 Good management of God's money means seeking first the kingdom of God. You do this by honoring God with a regular amount that you give as worship (the tithe principle) and giving additional offerings out of love and as God leads to help people in need. Your faith will be tested, but you will see how God will generously bless you when you give whatever He tells you to give. You can never give more than God, so obey Him in your giving of tithes and offerings.

Plan of Action

God's plan for you, His child, is that you ask Him to provide for every need as you give to Him tithes and offerings that are already His.

Receiving from God is part of your two-way relationship with Him—so it is always connected with your doing something as well. Your part in receiving God's provision of daily food is asking Him to provide and using your resources as you believe in your heart God wants you to use them. Review 2 Corinthians 9:7. Here are some steps to take to assist you in your new approach to money management:

1. Write out a simple budget to plan your regular use of income so you can be in control of your spending.

2. Include a regular amount—as often as you get paid—to give to God as worship. A tithe (one tenth of your income) is the best guideline for practicing this kind of giving as God commanded Israel to do. Pay the tithe amount first, and you will see that God makes the remaining nine tenths (if you spend it on needs and in giving to others' needs) go further than all of it did when you were managing things as if the money in your hands were actually your own.

3. List all of your basic needs and the amount needed for each thing.

4. Ask God to show you a monthly amount to give for spreading the gospel in other places.

5. Try to set aside some money for emergencies—yours or someone else's. Be alert for God's leading you to give for one-time needs (see Luke 10:33–35) Otherwise, spend only what you have budgeted. Avoid building up debt that will make you a slave to your creditors. Trust God according to the truths expressed in Philippians 4:11–13.

6. Discuss your budget with your Christian friend. Plan to report on how things are going as you and God manage His money together.

Your Daily Supply of Forgiveness

The world was stunned one crisp October day in 2006 when Charlie Roberts parked his milk truck outside the West Nickel Mines Amish school, walked inside, and gunned down ten little girls. Five died; five were terribly wounded with point-blank gunshot wounds to the head. Horrified, people searched for a motive, but only one emerged: the gunman had not forgiven God for the death of his daughter nine years earlier. Before shooting them, he told the Amish girls, "I'm angry at God, and I need to punish some Christian girls to get even with Him."

But what happened next stunned the world even more than the tragic shooting. The Amish community forgave the murderer and reached out in compassion to his family. A father and a grandfather of two of the girls expressed forgiveness only hours after the shooting. And an Amish neighbor visited the killer's devastated parents, putting his hand on their shoulders, telling them he loved them, and comforting them for an hour. More Amish than non-Amish mourned Charlie Roberts at his funeral, and the family of one little girl invited the Roberts family to their daughter's funeral. When donations came in to help the families with funerals and medical expenses, they shared with the Roberts family.

The world marveled at the forgiveness shown by the families when so greatly wronged. Roberts' family released the following statement:

"We are overwhelmed by the forgiveness, grace, and mercy that you've extended to us. Your love for our family has helped to provide the healing we so desperately need…. Your compassion has reached beyond our family, beyond our community, and is changing our world."

We must follow God's example of loving those who have hurt and wronged us.

Forgiveness isn't easy, but we must do it. The Bible commands it, and it's the only way to heal. Those who don't forgive others hurt themselves, those they love, and everyone around them. Forgiving others as God has forgiven us not only changes us—it changes the world.

Part 1

God loves sinners—people who have wronged Him.

 Read Romans 5:8.

A. God's first step in loving you was to arrange for your forgiveness.

    1. Read Romans 5:6–8. What did God do to make it possible for Him to forgive you?

    2. God shows His willingness to forgive by loving people even before they ask Him to forgive them. What are some of the ways He shows love to people who have not asked for forgiveness (Matthew 5:45)?

    3. Before Jesus died on the cross to make it possible for every person to be forgiven, how did He show that He is a friend of sinners (Matthew 11:19; Mark 2:13–17; Luke 15:1–2)?

B. Our first step in receiving God's love is receiving His forgiveness.

    1. God cannot give you His greatest blessings until after you have accepted His forgiveness. What are these greatest blessings (John 3:16–18; Ephesians 2:1–10)?

    2. After God initially forgives you, He continues to forgive you when you stumble and sin, are sorry, and ask Him to forgive you (Matthew 6:12; 1 John 1:9). You should ask God to forgive you at least every day / week / month (circle one). (Matthew 6:11 tells you to ask God every day for the food you need.) How often do you need forgiveness?

 God loves us and forgives us in spite of our many sins against Him.

Part 2

God commands you to love those who sin against you.

 Read Matthew 6:12.

A. Why does God want you to forgive those who wrong you?

   1. So you can be like your _____ (Matthew 5:43–48).

   2. Because God has _____ you (Matthew 18:21–35; Ephesians 4:32; Colossians 3:13).

   3. Because He has made it possible for you to forgive (Matthew 18:32–33).

B. What happens when you don't forgive those who wrong you?

   1. What happens to you (Matthew 6:14–15; Hebrews 12:14–15; Ephesians 4:26–27)?

   2. What happens to others around you (Hebrews 12:15)?

Forgiveness was necessary for you to come to God. Likewise, you must forgive others so you may stay with God (Matthew 6:14–15) and be healthy in your spirit (Hebrews 12:15).

 You must forgive others daily—for your own sake and for your ability to forgive others. God will freely forgive you if you ask often and forgive often.

Plan of Action

God's plan for you, His child, is for you to forgive those who have wronged you—as He has forgiven you for your sin.

A definition of forgiveness: to set aside an offense without any demand for

- revenge against your offender—getting even; or
- compensation from the offender—"you owe me."

Forgiveness requires loving people in spite of their wrongs against you. You must forgive whoever sins against you if you want to receive forgiveness from God (Matthew 6:15). Following are some helpful steps:

1. On a separate piece of paper, write the names of people you still have not forgiven and how they have wronged you.

2. Ask God to help you until you can decide to forgive them. Say each name and offense before God, committing to forgive each one.

3. Ask God to help you see those people's value in God's sight—to see them as precious to God and therefore precious to you. Remember their good points. Refuse to see them as entirely bad because of their offense. Remember, you are not entirely good either.

4. Remember how much God has forgiven—and continues to forgive—you. Picture yourself standing at the foot of the cross with that person with both of you receiving forgiveness through the death and love of Jesus.

5. To represent your release of these offenses and your desire for revenge or compensation, tear up or burn your list. Thank God that He has set you free to forgive—free from the prison of bitterness. Receive your freedom by faith!

6. Recognize that feelings of hurt and resentment are normal human reactions when people wrong us. Having these feelings is no more sinful than were Jesus' temptations in the desert—what you do with those feelings is what determines if you're doing right or wrong. The first step in surrendering such feelings to God is to own them. Admit to God that these particular feelings are indeed present and active in you. Or, you may need to ask or allow God to bring to the surface feelings you have been trying to ignore. These feelings often stop us from forgiving until we admit them and give them to God. You can proceed in faith knowing that God will not allow more feelings to surface than you can handle with His help (see 1 Corinthians 10:13). Whenever you recognize these negative feelings, you should confess your feelings to God and ask Him to forgive you for holding on to them. Then ask God to heal you from the wounds they have caused you.

7. Now begin praying that God will replace those feelings of hurt and resentment with the appropriate fruit of the Spirit needed to replace them—the healthy emotions supplied by the Spirit—much like healthy tissue that replaces diseased tissue when physical healing takes place. As a prayer re-

minder, put in writing the natural feelings you want to give up in exchange for the fruit of the Spirit—feelings you want to receive. Remember, these Spirit-supplied feelings will include recognizing how valuable your offenders are in God's sight as well as positive feelings of love toward them.

This does not mean that you will regard differently what they have done. When Jesus forgives us, He does not redefine our sin or pretend we are suddenly immune to sin. Real forgiveness is offered in response to real sin. Forgiveness also does not mean that you are suddenly able to fully trust the person in the area where he or she wronged you. Trust must be rebuilt in stages: a measure of risk is taken to extend a measure of trust. As each measure of trust is rewarded by faithfulness at that level, more trust can be extended. But the forgiver must risk trust beyond the level of faithfulness demonstrated by the offender. How much should you trust the offender at each level of rebuilding? Depend heavily on the leading of God's Spirit.

8. The evidence of emotional healing is being able to remember the experience of being sinned against without emotional pain at the memory. An offense can be forgiven while the memory is still painful. The pain (without resentment) is an indication that emotional healing is still needed even though real forgiveness has been extended.

Keep in mind that emotional healing is usually a process that happens over a period of time that varies depending on the depth of the need. Major healing events often come along with gradual healing from abiding in the Lord daily. Don't be discouraged when old hurts you thought had healed come to the surface. They will usually be weaker than before—showing that some healing has taken place but simply isn't yet complete. Don't feel condemned—just give those feelings back to God and ask for one more wave of healing by His Holy Spirit.

9. Where possible, do something that shows love for each person you have forgiven (Luke 6:27–28). This loving action, combined with continued prayer, will help bring the right feelings of love and compassion for the offender.

The right decision of your heart makes the forgiveness real—having the right feelings in your heart toward your offender shows that forgiveness is complete. When you can remember the offense without pain, you know the healing is complete. Persist until you are healed.

Reminder: Things to Do This Week

1. Pray each morning that God will give you a spirit of forgiveness. Look forward to the privilege of forgiving someone during the day, and then do it! At

the end of the day, thank God for each opportunity you had to forgive. Ask God to further bless the person you forgave.

2. Continue your daily quiet time study of Matthew 6:1–15, and work through Session 10 before your next meeting on:

This is a truly important session to understand and to respond to with an honest heart. What God will do in response to your honesty and effort will be life changing!

Freedom through Dependence

A local church's men's group decided they'd mentor younger men who seemed to need guidance in dealing with the challenges of genuine Christian living. One older man who had found the Lord late in life owned an auto repair shop where he employed a rather timid eighteen-year-old who had recently become a believer. The boy's father had been sick most of the young man's life, which left him timid and in need of fatherly influence.

One day at the shop, a customer arrived to reclaim his pickup truck—to be told that the truck was not ready due to problems uncovered that required additional repair work. The customer asked to see the boss and began loudly cursing and swearing about the unexpected delay. The young man watched with interest to see the boss's reaction. The boss chose to respond with the Lord's help:

By depending on God, you are free to live as God intends.

"Pardon me, sir, but every time I hear someone talk like that, it reminds me that I used to talk like that. But Jesus came into my life three years ago and cleaned up my mouth. Now whenever I hear this kind of talk, I have to stop and thank Jesus for what He has done for me. Hold on just a moment."

The boss looked upward and, eyes open, calmly said: "Jesus, You know I used to talk like this gentleman—but when You came into my life, You cleaned up my mouth and gave me a whole new way of talking. Just have to stop and thank You for that." The boss then looked at the customer and said, "Okay, sir, how can I help you?"

In response to the man's tirade, Satan was poised to inspire a sinful reaction and a bad example to the watching young man. However, the boss turned upward and allowed the Lord to determine his response. Righteous witness was given to the customer and helpful example to the young man. "Thy kingdom come" was fulfilled a little more that day.

Part 1

God will provide spiritual protection for you.

 Read Matthew 6:13.

A. When you're tempted, you are enticed to do wrong for pleasure or gain (James 1:14). You want to do or have something that God, in His loving wisdom, does not want for you.

1. You sin when you give in to temptation and offer yourself as a slave to impurity and wickedness to obey its demands (Romans 6:12, 19). James 1:14–15 explains it this way: "Temptation comes from our own desires, which entice us and drag us away. These desires give birth to sinful actions. And when sin is allowed to grow, it gives birth to death" (NLT).

2. Your natural self has many strong desires that are not God's will for you. Things you see, feel, and hear increase these desires. Study Galatians 5:16–21. What are some things that tempt you?

3. You are tempted when you see in your mind pleasurable reward for a sinful action that seems within your reach if you act now to get it. The desire for instant gratification hides the real meaning of the action and the results that will come later (James 1:15). You are deceived if you believe that trading short-term gain for long-term consequences is good for you. (What was Eve thinking when she committed the first sin, as recorded in Genesis 3:6?) Never forget or ignore the truth that sinful pleasure now always brings much grief and pain later.

4. Don't dwell on what tempts you. The longer you think about an immediate reward for sin and hold on to the desire to have it—the stronger your desire will grow and the weaker your will to resist grows. Avoid tempting situations or looking at things that bring sinful pleasures to mind, and you will find it easier not to sin. And whenever sinful pleasures do come to mind, replace them quickly by turning your mind to thoughts you know would please God. Memorize Philippians 4:8. What are two pleasures that strongly attract your natural self when you think about them? What will you do to safeguard yourself against them?

B. You can often avoid temptation. That's the reason for Jesus' words in Matthew 6:13.

1. You can often escape temptation by staying away from situations you know will stir your desire to sin. For example, if God has delivered you from alcohol, what kind of places should you not go, or what kind of situations should you avoid, to help yourself remain free of it?

2. When you cannot escape being in a place where there are tempting influences (for example, someone at your job who is sexually attractive), you can strengthen your heart and mind before you go there. Ask God to help you see that person through His eyes, as a person who is precious to God, rather than as an object for your mental or physical pleasure. Study God's Word (such as Matthew 5:28; Colossians 3:1–3; Romans 6:6, 11) and pray for the Spirit to make it powerful in you. When the tempting situation comes, instead of offering any part of yourself to sin and becoming a slave to its demands by giving in to temptation, exchange that action for the action commanded in Romans 6:13, 16, 19. Summarize what these verses teach you to do when tempted.

3. Ask God for the needed fruit of the Spirit (Galatians 5:22–23) to be at work in you when you need it. Write again the two pleasures that most strongly tempt your natural self. Then, for each one, write the fruit of the Spirit that would be a righteous replacement for that fruit of the flesh.

Temptations:	Fruit of the Spirit:

 Temptation seeks to entice you to sacrifice your long-term good for short-term pleasure. Giving in makes you a slave and leads to death (Hebrews 11:24–26).

Part 2

God rescues you from temptation and from spiritual attack.

Read Matthew 6:13.

A. Evil accurately describes the deception, slavery, and destruction brought by sin and Satan (John 8:44). Following are some major evils. Give some examples of each in the space provided.

   1. The bondage of sinful habits (Ephesians 2:1–3; 5:3, 18)

   2. The deception of wrong thinking (Ephesians 4:14, 17–19)

   3. Satan's harm (2 Timothy 4:16–18)

   4. Direct contact with evil powers (Ephesians 2:2; 6:12)

B. Jesus provides freedom from these evils (John 8:31–36; Ephesians 1:19–23).

   1. What is your part in this resistance or rescue operation? (See Matthew 6:13; Ephesians 6:10–20; James 4:7.)

   2. In the name of Jesus, dismiss from your life every evil spiritual power and activity you were involved with, and destroy any objects that went along with these practices (Deuteronomy 7:25–26). Read 1 John 4:4 and Ephesians 1:19–23, and don't be afraid!

 Romans 6:4–14; 8:31–39 is true. Act on this truth with faith and persistence. God promised victory, so don't stop until you've won.

Plan of Action

 God's plan for you, His child, is to depend on Him for spiritual protection.

1. "Rescue us from the evil one" (Matthew 6:13 NLT) is a battle cry of victory for the believer. Be careful to follow through on the promise in this line of your model prayer, the Lord's Prayer. Break away from Satan's power in your life and the evil activities that are chains of bondage. Some habits and demonic connections are not easy to break, but if you persist, God will help you be free of them. What is the promise of 1 John 4:1–4?

2. Do not be afraid of the evil one (Satan and his evil spirits), because he is no match for almighty God. Remember the end of the Lord's Prayer: "Thine is the kingdom, and the power, and the glory, forever. Amen" (Matthew 6:13 KJV). Also, remember Ephesians 1:19–22.

3. Steps to freedom:

    a. Describe any sinful activities or habits that still have a grip on you.

    b. Describe any contacts you still have with spiritual powers, objects, or practices—demonic games, Ouija boards, séances, idols, spiritualistic rituals, charms, fortune-telling, etc.

    c. Tell God you are sorry for your involvement in these things. Then act on James 4:6–8. The promises here are:

    The commands are:

    d. Read Ephesians 6:10–13; Psalm 2:3; Psalm 118:10–14; and Psalm 129:1–4 to strengthen your faith. Pray, guided by James 4:6–8, and resist the devil. In the name of Jesus—by His authority—break the powers of sin and Satan that have held you captive through bad habits, and dismiss the evil spirits that have had a grip on any area of your life. Speak to them directly in the authority of Jesus' name. Also, destroy any occult or magic objects (charms, idols, fortune-telling cards, etc.) you still possess. Whatever spiritual resistance you experience, don't back down! If you stand firm in God's strength, Satan will flee from you. Read 2 Corinthians 10:3–5.

    If you or your family are under any kind of covenant with satanic spirits (curse) entered into by you or previously by relatives or ancestors, break that curse by naming it and coming against it in Jesus' name. Use the words of Psalm 118:10–14 as your prayer. Where it says "all the nations" (verse 10), instead put in the name of the spiritual system or kind of spirit you have been linked with (such as witchcraft, masonry, occult group, false religion, etc.). Pray with confidence, "because the one who is in you is greater than the one who is in the world" (1 John 4:4). It is best to have a strong Christian friend or pastor pray along with you for these kinds of tough spiritual battles.

4. God is your rescuer and your refuge. He is greater than any evil practice or power you will encounter. Your heavenly Father will deliver you if you call on Him for help, continue to trust His power, and obey any instructions that He gives you in the process. Remember 1 John 4:4 and Ephesians 1:19–22, and live in peace and fellowship with God.

Reminder: Things to Do This Week

1. This unit truly deals with very important issues that affect your life. In coordination with Session 11, study Galatians 5:16–25 in your daily quiet time. Work through Session 11 before your next meeting on:

2. Look for a new way each day to depend on God.

Remembering Jesus Together

When three Ryan brothers were killed within days of each other during World War II, the military moved swiftly to extract from combat the family's sole surviving son, James Ryan. The 1998 blockbuster film Saving Private Ryan *tells the story of a special squad of soldiers assigned to locate James Ryan somewhere on the front lines at Normandy to keep one family from being entirely wiped out in serving their country. Captain John Miller heroically leads the squad on its dangerous mission. He saves Ryan, but at great cost, losing most of his men and being mortally wounded himself.*

As he lays bleeding and dying on a bridge in Normandy, Captain Miller addresses his poignant last words to the man he died to save: "James…earn this. Earn it."

When you take part in the Lord's Supper, come ready to remember the price He paid so you could come to the table.

At the movie's conclusion, we see an older James Ryan standing with his family at Captain Miller's grave. Ryan grapples with understanding the captain's enormous sacrifice—giving his own life to save Ryan's—and he contemplates whether his life has honored that great sacrifice. "Every day I think about what you said to me that day on the bridge," Ryan says. "And I've tried to live my life the best I could. I hope that was enough." In remembrance and gratitude, Ryan honors Miller's sacrifice by saluting his grave.

This memorable fictional story helps us understand the enormity of the real story of Jesus' sacrifice to save us. He sought us out behind enemy lines and made it possible for us to get "home" safely. He died so that we might live. All He asks in return is that we remember Him and honor His sacrifice when we partake of communion, or the Lord's Supper. "Do this in remembrance of me," Jesus commanded His followers at that first communion (1 Corinthians 11:24). And again, Jesus said: "Examine yourself before eating the bread and drinking the cup" so as to eat in a manner that is worthy or appropriate to His sacrifice for us (1 Corinthians 11:28 NLT).

If our heart is right toward Him, then we will live our lives submitted to His lordship. We need to examine our lives to assess the level of devotion evident in our attitudes and actions. We can never deserve our Lord's sacrifice for us, but we can love and appreciate Him sincerely and live lives of gratitude to Him for inviting us to His table and paying so dearly so He can have communion with us.

Jesus showed His disciples this special way of remembering after they ate the Jewish Passover dinner together the evening before He died. (The Passover was a special time each year for remembering and celebrating God's rescuing the Jews from slavery in Egypt. You can read the story in Exodus 11 and 12.) He gave His disciples communion to replace Passover because His followers can now celebrate deliverance from sin's slavery and eternal punishment. See Matthew 26:17–29 and 1 Corinthians 11:23–26.

 Read 1 Corinthians 11:23–30.

Part 1

 Communion helps us remember and honor Jesus for giving himself for us and to us.

 Read John 6:47–59.

A. Jesus said the communion bread was like His _____ provided for _____ (1 Corinthians 11:24).

1. Jesus took the bread and _____ it for the disciples to eat. This was symbolic of the breaking of His body in death to give life to those who would "eat" (John 6:51).

2. Jesus gave the disciples the broken bread, which they took and ate. Read 1 John 5:11–12, and review John 6:51, 57–58.

   a. A person must "take" or receive _____ to have eternal life (John 1:12).

   b. Eating the bread symbolizes Jesus' coming to live inside us, mixing together His life and our life in a close, ongoing relationship. In fact, the

one who eats the bread of communion should be responding to Jesus' presence as he or she is eating! This is the reason for the term *communion*, which speaks of our sharing in the life and presence of Jesus. The bread itself is just bread, but it is important in that it helps us remember Jesus' sacrifice for us.

3. Jesus told His disciples—including you—to "do this to remember me" (1 Corinthians 11:24 NLT) (literally, "be mindful of me") as they ate the broken bread. Jesus had given himself for them then but also now gives himself to His friends by being present with them always. That is why this ceremony is a time of present communion with Jesus around a symbolic dinner table.

B. Jesus said the cup of wine was like the new covenant (relationship) He was offering to mankind, paid for with His blood (1 Corinthians 11:25).

1. The cup of wine is a reminder that Jesus was crushed to release His life-purchasing blood. In what ways would wine be an appropriate symbol of Jesus' blood?

2. Jesus gave His disciples the cup, from which they all drank. Review Matthew 26:27–28 and John 6:53–56.

   a. One must enter into this covenant or new relationship and agree to follow whatever Jesus has planned, just as the disciples drank what Jesus had already put in the cup (1 Corinthians 11:25).

   b. Willingly drinking the cup speaks of willingly entering into a life-giving relationship with Jesus (John 6:54–56).

3. Jesus told His disciples—including you—to remember as they drank the cup that Jesus had poured out His blood for them then—but also being aware that He pours out His love to us now by being present with us always.

C. At the Lord's Supper, Jesus wants us to look with Him to the future (1 Corinthians 11:26).

1. As you share or have communion with Jesus at the Lord's Supper, what should you be thinking about besides Jesus (Matthew 26:29; 1 Corinthians 11:26)?

2. Read John 14:3; 1 Thessalonians 4:13–18; and 1 Corinthians 15:50–53. How and in what condition will we arrive at the place Jesus has prepared for us?

 When we eat the bread and drink the cup in the communion ceremony, we remember and honor the broken body and poured-out blood of Jesus in the past. In the present, we recognize and experience His presence with us as we participate.

Part 2

 We ought to examine ourselves before we eat of the bread and drink from the cup in the communion ceremony.

Read 1 Corinthians 11:28.

A. God is not satisfied with religious ceremony if a person is not sincerely worshiping from the heart. Read John 4:20–24.

The Bible says a person may be eating the bread and drinking the cup of the Lord in an unworthy manner (1 Corinthians 11:27). Note: The emphasis here is on the right manner or way in which a person should eat and drink—not on the person's worthiness of this privilege. The word *worthy* in the original language means "fitting" or "appropriate." Why is it wrong for a person to eat and drink in an unworthy manner? (Look again at 1 Corinthians 11:27.)

The right (fitting, appropriate) way of eating and drinking is to do it from the heart—sincerely remembering Jesus' death and responding to His presence now. Your actions should honor Jesus as the source and redeemer of your life. If you are truly honoring Him from your heart, then you are eating and drinking in a worthy manner. Why would it not be right for a nonbeliever to take part in this communion observance?

B. God will discipline a Christian who is eating and drinking for the wrong reasons (1 Corinthians 11:20–22, 27–32).

1. Some of the Corinthian believers were coming for the Lord's Supper but not thinking of the Lord (verse 20) or the other members of His body who had come to worship with them (verses 22, 29). From 1 Corinthians 11:21, 34, what does it seem they were thinking of instead?

2. How serious was their offense in God's eyes (1 Corinthians 11:27)?

3. God's judgment was not to reject them. What did God allow to happen to them and for what reason (1 Corinthians 11:30, 32)?

God's discipline should help us correct our behavior, which will then help us avoid the dangers of continuing in sin. Do you examine your own heart and life each day to see if anything in you might displease God?

C. Self-examination is an important part of the Christian life. (Think carefully about 1 Corinthians 11:31; 2 Corinthians 13:5.)

1. How can you avoid being disciplined by God (1 Corinthians 11:31)?

Some translations say we should "judge ourselves," which means to examine ourselves before the Lord to see if our thoughts and actions are right. If we do this by our own choice, God does not have to get our attention through discipline.

2. What then should you do before sharing in the communion ceremony (1 Corinthians 11:28, 31)?

3. When you examine yourself and discover some sin of thought or action, what should you do before taking part in the Lord's Supper? (See 1 John 1:9.)

4. Should you examine yourself only before taking part in the Lord's Supper? Why or why not?

 The Lord's Supper is a frequent occasion for you to carefully examine yourself before God. You should act according to 2 Corinthians 6:14–7:1. Then celebrate Jesus' sacrifice for you and His presence with you.

Plan of Action

The spiritual person evaluates everything, including—or especially—the self! Time for a check-up.

Use your quiet time each day this week to work on writing in your answers to the following personal review to help you evaluate your progress in getting to know God through learning to communicate and walk with Him. Discuss your answers with your friend when you and your friend both have plenty of time to talk.

1. Do you have deep and ongoing peace and security with your heavenly Father?

   a. Review your understanding of God's grace.

   • Review Ephesians 2:1–9 and write, in your own words, a definition of what it means to be saved by grace.

   • Do you feel like a beloved child of God as described in Ephesians 5:1; Romans 5:1, 5; 8:14–17? Explain.

   • How have you seen God keep His promises in your life?

   • Have you experienced God's blessing as described in Matthew 5:10–12 while being treated badly for being a Christian? Describe your experience.

b. Truly good actions are a result of God's grace in your life.

- Summarize in your own words the truth expressed in Ephesians 2:10.

- What good works have resulted from grace in your life?

Contract

Because of God's grace, you can go all out with Jesus (John 15:4–5, 14–15; Romans 8:12–39) without worrying about having to earn salvation. Be confident that God loves you always as His child—that His love is not based on how well you do each day. Your actions of obedience can and should be expressions of gratitude and love, not out of obligation or some misguided attempt to repay God for His goodness toward you. Prayerfully review Romans 8:12–17, 23–39.

　　Can you say without hesitation: "I have permanently joined myself with God through Jesus Christ and will stay with Him no matter what happens to me"?

Signed _____

Acts 11:23

2. How has your life changed since you became a Christian on _____ (date)?

a. Describe internal changes in you. Consider things like feelings of guilt and fear, values (use of time and money), thought life and attitudes, etc.

b. Describe changes in your relationships with people. Consider your ability to forgive; communication levels; and your interaction with family, non-Christian friends, persons in authority over you, enemies, and other Christians.

c. Describe your daily relationship with God.

- What is your view of God now as opposed to how you saw Him before you became a Christian?

- How has your worship changed and grown?

- How often do you remember God's presence and talk with Him? What do you say to God when you think of Him during the day?

- Have you heard God speak to you? About what?

- Do you obey these impressions in your heart or mind? What have been the results of this obedience?

- When do you have your daily quiet time? For how long?

  Benefits:

  Struggles:

Reminder: Things to Do This Week

1. Remember to discuss both sections of this personal review with your Christian friend. Be sure to thank God for what He has done in you and for you in the short time that He has been living in you.

2. Work through Session 12 before your next meeting with your Christian friend on:

Spiritual Living

BILLY
John William Hall
Born Jan 30, 1937—Died July 24, 1937
"He will wipe away every tear from their eyes.
There will be no more death or mourning or crying or pain,
for the old order of things has passed away."
Revelation 21:4

Cuba Hill and John Hall were missionaries whose singular devotion to God and His will took them separately to neighboring West African countries. They grew up on opposite coasts and left by cargo ship from New York City a week apart—John bound for Nigeria, and Cuba for Upper Volta (now Burkina Faso). They met in Africa and returned for furlough as husband and wife—a match made in heaven.

Soon they were blessed with a spunky little girl, Evelyn, and they returned to Upper Volta, where they pioneered the work in Ouahigouya, 110 miles north of the capital city of Ouagadougou. Soon little Billy arrived—healthy and full of smiles and life.

Cooperating with and depending on the Spirit means your day-to-day life will be holy.

When he was just four months old, Billy developed blackwater fever and dysentery, complicated by malaria. For two months, while fellow missionaries and African saints fervently prayed, the parents tenderly cared for their struggling baby with round-the-clock vigils, meager medical intervention, and fervent prayer of their own. At 3 a.m. on July 24, Billy's spirit left his little body and heartbroken parents—and was welcomed into heaven.

John and Cuba stood by the small casket and renewed their consecration to the Lord, asking Him to give them, in the place of their little darling, many souls born into the Kingdom. Cuba wrote to her parents: "Through it all, the Lord has been so good and has upheld us and sustained us. He means more to us than ever before, and there is a fresh longing in our hearts for His coming. Since our trust is in God

and we are serving Him, we haven't really lost our Billy—we shall have him again. The Lord is seeing us through."

John and Cuba Hall are a testimony of behavior that displays the fruit of the Holy Spirit within them. Obvious fruit included their continued love for God in spite of unanswered prayer for healing and for the Africans they came so far to serve. They demonstrated the fruit of peace that sustained them as they grieved the death of their child. The fruit of faithfulness kept them on site reaching Africans—whom they would continue to serve over a span of fifty-one years. They retired at age seventy-five and are now in heaven with Jesus and Billy. Their four surviving offspring rise up to call them blessed and give thanks for their heritage.

Part 1

Stay in touch and in step with the Spirit.

 Read Galatians 5:16, 25.

A. Speak often with Him, with all kinds of prayers (Ephesians 6:18).

B. Listen continually to hear the Spirit speak to you (John 15:4).

C. Believe that God will help you do what He says to do (Philippians 4:13).

D. Believe that God will do what He tells you to pray for (John 14:13).

E. Memorize God's promise and plan for you in Romans 8:28–29. Read on to the end of the chapter.

F. Be with other Christians often, at regular meetings and in between, to allow the Spirit to work in you through others, and through you to others. Carefully read Matthew 18:19–20 and Hebrews 10:23–25.

We are to live and walk by the Spirit. This means we must not go our own way and expect Him to come along behind. Rather, we should keep in step with Him as He leads us.

Part 2

The Holy Spirit lives in and acts through you to make you like Jesus.

A. Be like Jesus (Romans 8:29). Follow carefully the directions and examples from the Bible.

   1. Jesus lived the top two commandments: love God and love people (Matthew 22:38–40).

   2. The way Jesus lived is described in John 13:1–17; 21:1–14. Jesus lived in complete cooperation with the Holy Spirit, as described in Galatians 5:13–14, 22–23.

   3. Now consider the Holy Spirit's role in Jesus' life as described in Luke 4:18–19 and Acts 10:38. What or who was flowing out of Jesus?

   4. Read Galatians 5:22–23 to learn how you can live like Jesus with the Holy Spirit flowing out of you.

B. Cooperate with the Spirit. When you cooperate with Him, the Holy Spirit reproduces in your life Jesus' loving attitudes and actions. This is the fruit of the Spirit (Galatians 5:22–23)—what the Spirit produces in your life.

   1. According to Romans 5:5, from where does this fruit come?

   2. Make a list from Galatians 5:22–23. "The fruit of the Spirit is…"

   3. Which fruits have you seen most often in your life?

   4. Which ones seem weakest or don't appear often?

   5. In John 21:15–19 Jesus explained to Peter how to obey the top two commands to function as a pastor. In what ways did Peter need the fruit of the Spirit to accomplish what Jesus was saying he should do?

C. Recognize when your behavior is not from cooperating with the Spirit.

    1. List the behaviors described in Galatians 5:15, 19–21, 26 that were part of your life before you came to Jesus. List also the fruit of the Spirit.

Fruit of my natural self:	Fruit of the Spirit:

    2. Circle those behaviors you still find yourself doing. Place a check beside the one that is hardest for you to not do.

    3. Ask God to help you exchange these sinful behaviors for behavior (fruit) the Spirit will produce. Which kinds of spiritual fruit are needed to replace each kind of natural fruit that you listed under the fruit of your natural self? Draw lines to connect the natural fruit with its spiritual fruit replacement.

 "The heart is more deceitful than all else and is desperately sick; who can understand it" (Jeremiah 17:9 NASB). The human heart by itself can produce nothing but sin even when sincerely trying to do good (Romans 7:14–23). Only the Holy Spirit within you can produce fruit and behavior that is holy.

Part 3

Release the Holy Spirit to be holy and loving through you.

Read John 15:1–12.

A. You decide the winner of the battles inside of you (Galatians 5:16–17).

    1. Identify the two opponents squaring off against each other in Romans 5:17.

    2. You pick the winner of each battle by giving in to the desire of your _____ or by turning to the _____ to help you act His way.

B. Pray every day to win the battle for that day (John 15:7).

    1. Pray every morning, guided by Galatians 5:16, 22–25. Write down the guidelines for praying that you see in this passage.

    2. Pray specifically every morning for God to help you:

        a. Turn away from the desire to do what you listed under the fruit of your natural self (2.C.1.).

        b. Turn to the Holy Spirit to produce holiness through the fruit of the Spirit in your behavior, especially the fruit you listed as missing under 2.C.3.

    3. As you go through the day, silently ask God to help you respond with the fruit of His Spirit to each person and situation you encounter.

C. Depend on the Holy Spirit to win each battle (John 15:4–5; Romans 6:11–19).

    1. Turn away from sinful desires (Romans 6:11–13).

        a. Verse 11: Consider yourself to be _____ to sin, which makes it possible for you to do as described in verse 13.

        b. Verse 13: What does this verse give as the action that is the alternative to being dead to sin?

        Example: A natural thing to do when someone hurts you is to give yourself to anger, allowing it to direct and fuel your reaction. Play dead to such feelings and turn away from them and their influence so that you can…

    2. Turn to the Spirit.

        a. First, remember that you are considering yourself to be _____ to God and _____ to sin (Romans 6:11–12).

        b. Then, follow verse 13 and present yourself to God to receive instruction as to what to do next instead of doing what your natural self is urging you to do. All the members of your body are alive from the dead (ready for action), and are ready to be instruments or tools of _____ as directed by God (Romans 6:13).

        Note: The pattern of this action is familiar. You've had a lot of practice with allowing strong feelings—such as anger—to guide and provide

energy for your actions. Now just change the direction you turn. Turn to the Holy Spirit and give in to His influence. He will help you respond with the fruit—the character—of the Spirit as Jesus did. Write in your own words the instructions in Romans 6:19.

Example: When you are angry, you should turn away from the temptation to react in anger and instead present yourself to God to release the Spirit-fruit or fruits of _____ to operate instead of anger.

 The fruit of the Spirit needed for a holy response is available to you when you turn to the Holy Spirit in any situation. The more you allow the Spirit's responses to replace your natural reactions, the more you will have and demonstrate to other people the character and love of the Spirit. To help your heart beat along with God's heart, follow the Plan of Action below.

Plan of Action

God's plan for you, His child, is to live a life of holiness.

1. Stay alert to the Holy Spirit. This is essential for releasing the fruit of the Spirit (John 15:4–5). As you continue your walk by the Spirit (Galatians 5:16, 25), make every activity of business, study, conversation, planning, or pleasure a joint project or shared experience with God. *I* has now become *we*. Life has no more private experiences. Sharing them all with God gives them much greater value to you and to God. God has promised to guide you and provide for you in whatever way you need, but your mind and heart must stay attentive to God.

Remember, John 10:4 and Romans 8:14 are both promises and commands. As you stay tuned in, you will hear His voice. And the more you obey the voice of God in your heart and through His Word, the sharper your spiritual hearing will become, the more His power will flow through you to help you obey, and the sweeter will be your fellowship with God.

2. Ask God to help you have His heart for people, demonstrated by:

   a. Eyes that see needs. According to Matthew 9:36, what need did Jesus see?

b. Real concern for people with needs. In Matthew 9:36, how do you know Jesus was concerned for the people?

Psalm 126:5–6: "He that sows in _____ shall reap with _____."

Rewrite John 11:33–35 in your own words.

In Acts 20:31, what did Paul have plenty of as he cared for people?

c. Willingness to enter their needy, painful world…

- In prayer. Read Matthew 9:38. Rewrite Galatians 4:19 and Colossians 4:12–13 in your own words.

- In service. Rewrite 2 Corinthians 3:3 and 1 Thessalonians 2:7–12 in your own words.

Reminder: Things to Do This Week

1. Resume your daily quiet time, studying Galatians 5:19–25 and completing your Daily Journal.

2. Complete Session 13 before your next meeting on:

Part 4

In addition to simple serving, God also blesses others through us with GIFTS OF THE SPIRIT

A. **SPIRITUAL SERVICE GIFTS:** In addition to simple acts of unskilled serving that meet simple needs (e.g. Jesus washing feet), God meets more challenging and ongoing needs through "gifts of the Spirit" given through His servants to people in need. These "gifts" or blessings are usually delivered by a combination of God-created abilities and empowerment by the Holy Spirit, and often are delivered through ONGOING MINISTRIES, (e.g. teaching, and mercy ministries).

God gives various gifts through different persons, so all members need to exercise their gifts to meet the different needs in the body (I Cor.12:29; Eph.4:11-12,16; I Peter 4:10). Sound and sober SELF-APPRAISAL is prescribed for each of us to identify God's gifts through us. (Rom.12:3,6; I Tim.4:16) Ask yourself the question: "What is God giving me faith and ability to do?" (I Peter 4:10-11) Then ask God the same question.

B. **EQUIPPING GIFTS:** In Ephesians 4:11-12, the Apostle Paul lists as gifts to the church individuals with five different functions or roles who also have the assignment of equipping believers "for the work of the ministry". This would include helping believers identify, develop and exercise their giftings for effective ministry.

IDENTIFY AND EXERCISE GIFTS OF THE SPIRIT (Rom. 12)

1. The gifts God chooses to give through us are stirred up and discovered as we focus on the needs of others. A servant's heart is essential to identify our spiritual service gifts and exercise them with humility. If we are not caringly involved in the lives of others, there will be no God-pleasing reason to discover and develop the abilities He has given us to meet needs that other people have. The more we concentrate on the needs of those around us, the more the Holy Spirit will be free to work through our spiritual gift(s) to meet those needs. (I Thess. 1:5)

2. Each spiritual gift inclines its possessor to notice certain kinds of needs and overlook others. A prophet, for example, may see sin in another's life and wonder why a server seems to overlook it. A server often will see unmet needs and wonder why a prophet doesn't see them. Ask yourself what kinds of needs you notice in others and feel motivated to help meet. That will often help you identify your spiritual gift(s). And don't be critical of others who don't see the same needs you see.

3. When a believer properly exercises a spiritual gift, there will be fruitfulness. When believers try to exercise their spiritual gift in a fleshly or carnal manner, there will often be reaction or misunderstanding from intended recipients. Reflecting on misuses often provides a helpful confirmation of what a person's gift really is – while also revealing the need for a greater dependence on the Spirit in delivering one's gift.

4. Observing those who are exercising/delivering their gifts fruitfully can provide helpful insight for growth in exercising one's own spiritual gifts and spiritual fruit.

Fill in Appendix 4: "SURVEY OF SPIRITUAL SERVICE GIFTS" for assistance in identifying yours. Consult with church leaders for assistance in being trained for and connected to a ministry where you can begin to develop and deliver your service gifts to others who need them.

Going with the Flow

Painful as it was to lose their infant son, John and Cuba Hall— missionaries to Burkina Faso, West Africa—determined that they would not quit doing what God had called them to do. They trusted in the Lord and leaned on Him in their sorrow.

They noticed that the Africans were watching them closely, and after a while, many of them began asking questions. Infant mortality is so high in West Africa that nearly everyone has lost one or more children. For them, death is devastating because they have no hope for the future. When someone dies, family and friends wail and scream and beat their chests in despair because they believe the evil spirits have come and stolen their loved one's soul away.

When people saw that the Halls did not mourn like that, they wanted to know why. It gave them many opportunities to tell about Jesus, His sacrifice for them, and that His death and resurrection conquered death and gives assurance of eternal life. Only eternity will show how many souls were won for the kingdom of God as a result of Billy's death.

John and Cuba found new meaning in 2 Corinthians 1:3–4, where the apostle Paul wrote: "Praise be to the God and Father of our Lord Jesus Christ, the Father of compassion and the God of all comfort, who comforts us in all our troubles, so that we can comfort those in any trouble with the comfort we ourselves have received from God." The Halls praise God for the comfort they received that allowed them to give comfort to others.

Billy's death appeared to be a calamity and brought great sorrow to his grieving parents. However, God's divine purpose was accomplished through his early departure. The Spirit worked through the Halls, powerfully increasing their witness to the saving truth of Jesus Christ. This is an example of moving in the flow of the Spirit—working *with* the Spirit in Jesus' name, not merely working *for* Jesus. Witness to Jesus requires supernatural power

Pray for more workers, and for great effectiveness in their work.

along with human effort to follow the instruction of the Spirit and God's written Word (Acts 1:8). Pray for workers who will flow with power—and keep in the flow yourself. The potential harvest is great, and workers full of the Spirit's power are the key (Matthew 9:38).

 Read Acts 1:8.

Part 1

 God gives ability from above for workers to be effective in doing His work on earth.

 Read John 1:32–34; 16:7–15.

A. Jesus himself relied on this ability from above to be effective in ministering to others.

1. Luke 4:18—"The _____ of the Lord is _____ me, because he has anointed me."

2. Acts 10:38—"God anointed Jesus of Nazareth with the _____ and _____, and…he went around doing good and healing…because God was with him."

B. Just before returning to heaven, Jesus talked to His disciples about this help from above.

1. What did Jesus tell them to wait for (Acts 1:4–5)?

2. Who would baptize them in the Holy Spirit (John 1:33–34)?

3. In Acts 1:6–9, Jesus told His followers:

a. What would happen. (Describe it here.)

b. What they would become. (Summarize it here.)

c. Where they would do this. (Define their mission field here.)

4. According to Luke 24:49–53 and Acts 1:13–14, what did the disciples do in Jerusalem?

C. After the Holy Spirit was poured out on them, the disciples became Christ's witnesses. Read the exciting story in Acts 2 through 4. (Note: Being filled with the Spirit is the same as being baptized in the Spirit. When a person is baptized in the Holy Spirit, he or she receives ability from God to say and do things he or she could never do alone—which shows that God's power is working through that person.)

1. New abilities. Read Acts 2:4, 6, 11, 14–18, 36–41. What did the Holy Spirit do through people and in people on the Day of Pentecost?

2. New power. Read Jesus' promise in Mark 1:16–18: "I will make you _____ of men." How does Acts 4:31 show this happening?

3. Changed lives. Peter experienced a big change in his life.

a. Describe Peter before he was filled with the Spirit (John 13:36–38; 18:1–27).

b. Describe Peter after he was filled with the Spirit (Acts 4:13; 5:17–32). What can you tell about Peter's change of character by what he wrote in 1 Peter 3:8–17?

4. Continuing mission. Read about other Christians in the early church who were filled with the Spirit (Acts 4:31; 8:14–17; 9:17; 10:44–47; 13:52; 19:1–6). Notice the things they did as they were controlled by (filled with) the Spirit.

a. According to Acts 2:39, who does God want to have this experience of being filled with the Spirit?

b. Does this mean you, too? Do you want to be filled with the Spirit? Explain.

 You are baptized in the Holy Spirit the first time you surrender to the Spirit so deeply that He gives you words of praise to God in a language you don't know—and you actually say them out loud. This gives you faith to surrender again and again, receiving ability from God to say and do things you could never do alone (Acts 1:8). This allows people to see Jesus at work through you. As Jesus' witness, you will do and say the things Jesus did and said. And you will tell who Jesus is and how He arranged for us to be with Him forever.

Part 2

You can receive this ability from above.

A. Prepare to receive.

1. Jesus wants you to receive power so that you can be what? (Read Acts 1:8.) Do you want more power—the ability—to tell other people about Jesus?

2. Read John 7:37–38. Jesus invites you to come to Him and drink if you are spiritually thirsty for more. How thirsty are you? Explain.

3. Jesus wants your complete surrender, and you want rivers of living water to spring up inside of you, giving you power to be His witness. Ask Jesus to show you anything you are holding on to in your life that hinders you from being baptized in the Holy Spirit and what you should do about it. Then do it. Write what needs to change and how the Holy Spirit directs you to make the needed change. Copy what you write to a prayer list for daily reference.

B. Pray in faith that you will receive (Luke 11:9–13).

1. Ask Jesus to baptize you in His Holy Spirit (John 1:33). Your part is to surrender completely so the Spirit can take control.

2. Now begin to praise Jesus with joy (Luke 24:52–53) because He has saved you and is going to baptize you in His Spirit. You know He will, because He promised He would in Acts 2:38–39. So go ahead and thank Him!

3. As you praise Him, concentrate completely on Jesus the baptizer. He will make you know (give you faith) that if you will begin to speak, the Spirit will give you His words. (Acts 2:4 says the believers gathered were all filled with the Holy Spirit and began to speak in other languages as the Spirit enabled them.) When the faith comes to you that you can speak with words supplied by the Spirit, begin to speak—but don't use your own words. Just say the words the Spirit gives you. Because it's a new experience, you may feel awkward—but just relax and let the new praises flow. Praying this way will soon feel natural.

4. If there is a delay in your being filled, don't be discouraged. God is delighted in your coming. Go back to point A.3, surrender yourself to Him, and keep seeking.

5. This experience is a beginning…so continue it daily—and powerfully!

 Being filled with the Spirit and speaking a new language is impossible to do on our own. Jesus is the one who baptizes you in the Holy Spirit. Prepare to receive, pray to receive, and then power up.

Plan of Action

God's plan for you, His child, is to become a worker in His harvest with the Holy Spirit's help.

1. You can pray to be baptized in the Spirit when you are alone—but don't hesitate to ask others to pray with you. Keep in mind that God delights in every sincere move you make toward Him, so don't be discouraged by delays. He has promised to baptize you in His Spirit—"The promise is for you and your children and for all who are far off—for all whom the Lord our God will call" (Acts 2:39). That includes you, so go on seeking until you are filled—not with worry but with genuine thirst for God and confidence in the outcome.

2. Keep in mind that being baptized in the Spirit is not the end or even the highest point of your spiritual journey. God intends it to be the beginning of a Spirit-powered life in which you witness about Jesus' love and see the lost transformed by that love. You should be praying in a Spirit-given language frequently, and you should be stepping out daily in the flow of the Spirit to help people around you put their faith in Christ.

3. Memorize the F-L-O-W outline below that explains Acts 1:8. Use it as a prayer guide and plan for witnessing and harvesting.

a. Faith in God (God-confidence that overcomes fear—Acts 4:29–30)

- Alert to the Spirit leading you to nonbelievers
- Trusting the Spirit to work through you and in them

b. Love from God

- His love coming to me for others through His Spirit within (Romans 5:5)
- His love being released through me to others (fruit of the Spirit: Galatians 5:22–23)

c. Openings by God

- Looking for doors opened by the Spirit for witnessing (Colossians 4:2–6)
- Opening my mouth with boldness from the Spirit (Ephesians 6:19–20)

d. Winning the nonbeliever to faith in Christ (2 Corinthians 3:2–6) by the Spirit's drawing (John 12:32)

- Gaining the nonbeliever's trust as a friend through kindness and listening
- Persisting until the nonbeliever's trust is placed in Jesus (Matthew 16:16–17)

Note: Peter's confession was by revelation, not by human observation—in spite of how close Peter was to Jesus.

 Without the Spirit, we cannot succeed in the harvest—but in the F-L-O-W of the Spirit, we cannot fail.

Reminder: Things to Do This Week

In your quiet time study each day, make notes on the F-L-O-W in Acts 1 through 12.

Sowing Gospel Seed

A friend brought a recently released felon to a pastor to hear the good news of Jesus. The pastor told the man that Jesus had died on the cross for his sins, and he urged him to ask forgiveness for those sins. That news sounded good to the felon, but he struggled to understand how it could work for him. Then a thought occurred to him: "Pastor, do you mean that Jesus took the rap for me?" The pastor agreed that was exactly what Jesus had done. He was then able to lead the man to a faith commitment to Jesus, who truly had taken the rap for him on the cross.

Missionaries arrive on foreign soil realizing that they must translate the good news into the local languages for people to understand and be saved. The same principle is essential within subcultures and differing life experiences even when people speak the same official language. The apostle Paul realized this and adapted his vocabulary and approach to fit the mind-set of his listeners. (See 1 Corinthians 9:19–23 and Acts 17:16–33.) Paul even asked the Colossians to pray that he would be able to make the good news clear to his various listeners, and he encouraged the Colossians to know how to respond to each person when they witness (Colossians 4:3–6). This principle applies in modern Western society as well. When we translate the unfamiliar truth into familiar terms, people who hear us can understand, and Satan is not allowed to steal it away.

We should know the truth that each hearer needs to understand—and also prepare ourselves to explain it clearly in the vocabulary of the individuals who stand before us. This will enable them to know the truth and be saved.

This session contains the essential truth of the gospel with clarity regarding what lost people need to know to be found.

Part 1

God loves you and wants you to be close to Him as His child— now and forever.

 Read John 1:12, Romans 8:15–17.

God's whole plan for your life with Him—as His child—is described in the following three activities you should continue to do:

A. Receive God's love through faith in Jesus Christ (John 3:16).

    1. Put your faith in Jesus, and then believe that His Spirit has come to live *in* you and is giving you God's life and love (Romans 5:5; 8:9–11).

    2. Receive through Jesus the provision of your needs—forgiveness, guidance, the ability to obey God, and material supply—by His Spirit (Matthew 6:33; John 15:4–5).

B. Respond to God with sincere love and worship (Luke 10:27).

    1. Repent of sin and be thankful for His love (Acts 2:38; 1 John 4:19).

    2. Depend on His Spirit in everything you do and for everything that you need (John 15:4–5, 14).

C. Release God's love through you to other people (Luke 10:27).

    1. Forgive and love others from your heart as you are forgiven and loved by God (Luke 10:27, 33; 11:4).

    2. Show love to people in actions and words by cooperating with the Holy Spirit (Luke 10:34–37; Galatians 5:22–23).

God's whole plan for your life with Him as His child is in the three activities described above. To help you remember, write in the missing words to complete the following outline:

1. _____ God's love through _____ .

2. _____ to God with _____ .

3. _____ God's love through _____ .

Part 2

You can become God's beloved child and have this wonderful life trusting Jesus as your sacrifice (sin payment), your Savior (helping friend), and your Lord (leader).

 Read Romans 10:12–13.

 Read John 3:16; 1:12; 15:14 and then follow these steps:

A. Ask Jesus to forgive you, and accept Him as your sacrifice, your sin payment (John 3:16).

   1. Believe that Jesus' suffering and death was full payment of the penalty for your sins, so you don't have to pay for them forever in hell (Matthew 20:28; John 1:29).

   2. Trust Jesus to forgive you of your sins so you won't go to hell for being a sinner and so your life now will not be controlled by sin (John 3:16; Romans 8:1–4).

B. Believe in Jesus as your living Savior and your helping friend forever (John 1:12; 15:14).

   1. Believe that Jesus rose from death to life and is now able to give you eternal life as God's child (John 1:12; Romans 6:21–23).

   2. Trust Jesus to put His Spirit in you and to help you with everything you need for your life (John 8:31–36; Romans 8:8–11, 35–39).

C. Cooperate each day with Jesus as your leader and Lord (John 15:14; Romans 6:22).

   1. Believe in Jesus' purpose and plan for your life on earth (Luke 9:24; Romans 8:28).

   2. Trust Jesus as your leader by cooperating with Him in everything you do (Luke 9:23; Romans 8:13–14).

 When you receive Jesus, you are born of the Spirit (John 3:5). You become a member of God's family and begin a whole new life—forgiven and able to experience God's provision and the blessings of cooperation with God—for eternity.

To help you remember how a person becomes God's child through Jesus Christ, write in the missing words:

A_____ _____ from Jesus, your s_____ (sin payment).

B_____ in Jesus as your living S_____ (helping friend).

C_____ each day with Jesus as your L_____ (leader).

Now memorize this simple outline (Sacrifice, Savior, Lord) and the three main Bible verses (John 3:16; 1:12; 15:14). It will be a great help to you in sharing the gospel with lost people.

This material will prepare you to clearly share the good news as you follow the leading of the Spirit in reaching out to lost people.

Remember that a clear explanation needs to be accompanied by a clear example of Christian character. The fruit of the Spirit should be evident in your life.

According to the Bible, the primary reason for salvation is to bring people into fellowship with God—not just to rescue them from hell. A new believer needs to combine faith and effort each day in his or her spiritual childhood to learn how to live in continual fellowship with God as outlined in Part 1. Keep in view that the goal of evangelism is to bring people into an ongoing relationship with God through Jesus Christ, not just a brief encounter with God. Study the next session carefully to learn how to help a nonbeliever begin and continue to live in fellowship with God.

Write in the missing words from John 14:6. Jesus said, "I am the _____, the _____, and the _____. No one _____ to the Father [God], except _____ me." Do you understand what Jesus said well enough to be able to explain it to someone else?

Plan of Action

God's plan for you, His child, is to reach out with the good news about Him to lost people.

1. Pray with your Christian friend for specific people you are witnessing to—that God will help you lead them to Him.

2. Carefully choose a few nice-looking tracts that also have a clear message similar to what you have learned in this unit. Give them to people you meet. Be sure to give them with love and a smile.

3. A person who wants to become a Christian often needs help putting his or her commitment to God into words in prayer. Write out and memorize a faith commitment prayer so you will be ready when God gives you opportunity to lead someone to Him. Your preparation will be a step of faith that God will, in fact, give you this opportunity to help someone give his or her life to God. Use the "ABC—Sacrifice, Savior, Lord" outline as a guideline for writing a faith commitment prayer that is faithful to the gospel message. After you have written it, review it and see if you have included all the basic elements that a person needs to know to decide to make a serious, lasting commitment to Christ. Here is a sample prayer:

Jesus, I believe that You are the Son of God and that You died to pay for my sins against You. I am sorry for my sins, and I ask You to forgive me.

Jesus, I believe that You rose from the dead, and I ask You to come live in me and be my friend forever. I believe You will provide eternal life as God's child and whatever I need each day.

Jesus, I believe that You have the best purpose and plan for my life. I want to cooperate with You as my leader and depend on Your help for everything I do. Thank You for loving me so much that You have made my heart Your home. I love You, Jesus. Amen.

You might also share with this new spiritual baby in the family that he or she needs continuous contact with God to have continual conduct with God.

4. In Session 15 you will learn how to use the information you learned in this session. These last two sessions are extremely important for you to learn well and remember long. Other people's eternal lives depend on your being well equipped to lead them to Christ. So please put forth extra effort to study thoroughly these long sessions—for the sake of the lost people around you. Keep in mind that you are studying for their sake, not just for yourself. And use Ephesians 6:19–20 as a guide for your praying.

Reminder: Things to Do This Week

Work through Session 15 for the study part of your daily quiet time. Session 15 is especially long and important to understand, remember, and practice continually. Be thorough in discussing this unit with your Christian friend when you meet on:

Reaping

In his teen years, Dawson Trotman spent his energies gambling and pursuing other youthful pleasures in his home city of Los Angeles. At age eighteen he began courting Lila, a pretty girl whose first love was Jesus. She wouldn't associate with Dawson unless he attended her church. At his first church meeting, Dawson was assigned six Bible verses to memorize. At the second meeting, Dawson was the only one who had memorized them all. The same thing happened at the third meeting. While trying to impress Lila, the truth he was taking in took him in, and he began a personal relationship with the author of the words he'd memorized.

His experience convinced Daws that memorizing the Bible was the key to having a strong Christian faith. He also became passionate about personally introducing others to the Jesus he had met in the Scriptures. He began to organize youth groups and hand out scores of Scriptures to be memorized. One day in 1934, a mother asked him to visit her son, a sailor.

The sailor and Daws sat in his old car near the dock, and Trotman quoted the Bible to the young man until a policeman became suspicious. Trotman talked the officer into joining them for prayer. The young sailor said: "I'd give my right arm if I could do what you just did." That sailor led a friend to Christ with the approach he learned from Trotman, and that new believer in turn convinced another. Dawson's movement, eventually known as Navigators, spread across the seven seas—at one point during the war having a presence on more than a thousand ships and stations. With the help of converted sailors reentering society along with a partnership with the Billy Graham crusades, Navigators grew and eventually included multitudes on land worldwide.

Notes

This session will help prepare you to be sent into your world to advance God's kingdom by increasing its citizens and the level of their service to the King.

Upon learning of Trotman's death, Billy Graham spoke for many Christians in many places of the world: "I think Daws has personally touched more lives than anybody I have ever known.... He lived to save others."

Along with many Navigators, you have benefitted from being mentored in your new faith in Jesus. This experience has prepared you to be a mentor to serious inquirers and to other new believers. As Jesus commanded, pray that the Lord of the harvest will send workers into His harvest (Matthew 9:35–38). Then volunteer to be part of the answer to your prayer. Will you say to the Lord of the harvest, "Here am I, Lord, send me"?

 Read John 4:35–36.

Part 1

Teamwork between believers and the Lord of the harvest is the process for reaping.

Following are the visible and invisible phases through which a nonbeliever passes on his or her way to new B-I-R-T-H. The Holy Spirit and the cooperating laborer work together in each phase. It is helpful to find where a lost person is to know what the next phase is on his or her journey.

A. **B**ridge—a Spirit-arranged contact that inspires interest and trust in the non-believer toward the laborer, allowing further contact for witness (John 4:7; Acts 8:26–31; Acts 10:19–20)

　1. The laborer makes contact as prompted or arranged by the Spirit.

　2. The Spirit begins by preparing the nonbeliever's heart and then arranges contact with the laborer.

B. **I**nsight—a sinner's God-given recognition of sin, separation from God, and the need for forgiveness (John 16:8)

　1. The laborer helps the nonbeliever recognize and admit his or her need. The laborer identifies the needs by observation, inquiry, or revelation from the Spirit.

　2. The Spirit convinces the nonbeliever of his or her need.

C. Revelation—when the nonbeliever knows in his or her spirit that the gospel is true (Matthew 16:17)

1. The laborer explains the content of the good news, clarifying that Jesus must have authority over our daily lives (Romans 10:14).

2. The Spirit convinces the nonbeliever that the good news is, in fact, true.

D. Trust—when the nonbeliever repents of sin and puts his or her faith in Jesus Christ (Romans 10:9–13)

1. The Spirit influences the nonbeliever to choose to give in to God's love (Acts 16:14). Unless prompted otherwise by the Holy Spirit, generally the witness should see evidence that the Spirit is drawing a person before encouraging the nonbeliever to trust Jesus.

2. When it is evident that the Spirit is drawing the nonbeliever toward a faith commitment, in a gentle, nonpressuring way, the laborer invites and encourages the nonbeliever to pray to put his or her trust in Jesus as their leader and friend. If the nonbeliever agrees to do so, the terms of the contract should be reviewed and the nonbeliever encouraged to pray his or her own commitment prayer. If the person wants your help in praying, help as explained below. Avoid pressuring the nonbeliever into a premature birth (Matthew 13:20–21). If you do assist people in praying a commitment prayer:

   a. Explain that it is their prayer if they mean it from their heart.

   b. Keep the words simple and common so they can understand immediately and easily make what you say their own prayer. (It is helpful to have a commitment prayer in everyday language already prepared.)

   c. Make the prayer easy to follow by leading slowly and using brief phrases.

   d. Lead in a prayer that is not too short (omitting essentials) or too long (tiring or confusing to the person).

E. Home—the new believer is born of the Spirit when the Holy Spirit comes to live in the new believer, who now belongs to God as His child. God is now Father, and other Christians are brothers and sisters.

1. The laborer accepts the newborn as a brother or sister and rejoices in God's grace.

2. The Spirit of adoption enters the new believer and becomes the spiritual connection with God and other spiritual family members.

3. Older family members disciple the new member in how to live as a member of the family of God.

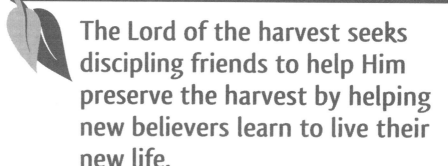 God activates each B-I-R-T-H stage during the conversion process. Be observant and alert through the Spirit to recognize each stage and cooperatively follow His lead as you labor with Him (John 5:19).

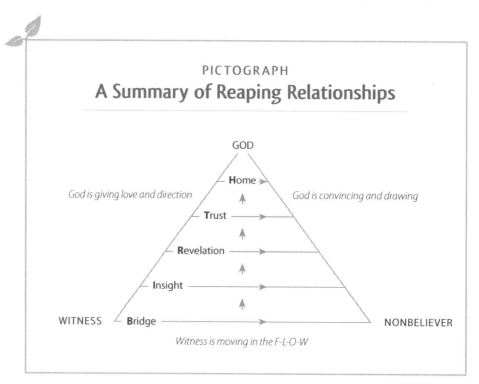

PICTOGRAPH
A Summary of Reaping Relationships

GOD

God is giving love and direction   *God is convincing and drawing*

← **Home** →

Trust →

Revelation →

Insight →

WITNESS   **Bridge** →   NONBELIEVER

Witness is moving in the F-L-O-W

Part 2

The Lord of the harvest seeks discipling friends to help Him preserve the harvest by helping new believers learn to live their new life.

A. The new believer needs a friend to L-O-V-E him or her with God's love (1 Thessalonians 2:7–8). Here's how:

1. **L**ike the new believer—show warmth.

2. **O**pen your life to the new believer for a two-way friendship.

3. **V**alue the new believer as a brother or sister and as a precious child of God.

4. Encourage the new believer to stay faithful in contact and conduct with God (Acts 11:23).

B. The new believer needs a discipler to H-E-L-P him or her learn to walk with God (1 Thessalonians 2:9–12; 4:1–2).

1. **H**ear—really listen to—the new believer to understand him or her.

2. **E**xplain the truth in terms the new believer can understand, in response to questions and needs, using the sessions in *THRIVE*.

3. **L**ead the new believer by example, practical instruction, encouragement, and accountability.

4. **P**ray for the new believer daily and diligently.

 A Discipling Friend who L-O-V-Es a new believer will H-E-L-P him or her learn to walk with God. A church family that loves its new members will joyfully receive them, value them, and help them become a functioning part of the body of believers.

Part 3

The Lord of the harvest seeks more workers.

Read Matthew 9:37–38.

A. Only people who have been harvested can be workers (Acts 4:20). They can:

1. Share the message with full conviction that it is true (1 Thessalonians 1:5).

2. Explain the message from personal experience (1 Thessalonians 1:5; 2:10).

B. Workers are people who pray (Matthew 9:38; Ephesians 6:19). They pray:

1. That the Lord of the harvest will send out workers (Matthew 9:38).

2. For themselves as they obey His command to go (Mark 16:15; Acts 1:8).

   a. For words that are _____ (Colossians 4:3–4, 6).

   b. For conduct that is _____ (Colossians 4:5).

c. For a manner that is _____ (Ephesians 6:19–20).

3. For an _____ door for witness (Colossians 4:3).

4. For God's help in _____ the opportunity (Colossians 4:5).

C. Workers cooperate with God as they labor. Review how Jesus cooperated with the Father by reading John 5:17–20; 8:28; 4:35–38.

1. Cooperative workers are alert to what the Spirit is doing in a nonbeliever (John 5:19).

   a. They know the steps the Spirit takes to draw a person to himself—as outlined under B-I-R-T-H.

   b. They are observant of circumstances (like the good Samaritan—Luke 10:33).

   c. They are good listeners who seek knowledge through conversation (as with Philip and the Ethiopian—Acts 8:30–37).

   d. They are sensitive to revelation from the Spirit (see John 4:17–18; Acts 8:26; 16:9–10, 18).

2. Cooperative workers act in partnership (cooperation) with the Spirit.

   a. They respond to obvious needs according to the principles of God's Word unless directed otherwise by the Spirit (as did the good Samaritan—Luke 10:34–35).

   b. They are led by the Spirit in ways that are unexpected in the natural view of things (as with Philip and the Ethiopian—Acts 8:26, 29; and Peter and Cornelius' household—Acts 10:19–20).

Plan of Action

God is sending you, His child, to work with Him to gather the harvest.

1. Have you been sent by the Lord of the harvest?

a. To whom?

b. To do what?

c. Does your heart beat with God's heart—full of love for lost people? Are you constantly praying for God to give you His love?

2. How would you evaluate your obedience in witnessing and discipling new Christians?

a. Strongest areas:

b. Weakest areas:

3. Find a Bible passage to guide your praying for each of the weak areas listed above. Make a prayer list, writing each need area followed by the Bible passage that speaks to that need. Leave space beside each item to write in answers to prayer as they come.

Prayer List Sample

Need: Lack of love for the lost

Prayer: Matthew 9:36 (NASB): "Seeing the people, He felt compassion for them." Lord, help me to see people's needs and feel Your love for them.

Answer: (Write how God is giving you His love for people you know, and give their names.)

 ## Prepare for a lifetime of winning people to Jesus.

1. Prayerfully review the F-L-O-W progression in Session 13, giving close attention to the two points under each letter. Write the outline on a sheet of paper, and put it in your Bible or prayer notebook to use as a frequent guide for praying. Plan regular times to pray through this outline on a daily or weekly basis.

2. Memorize the B-I-R-T-H outline and the two points under each letter, a job-description for the Holy Spirit and you. Rehearse it with a friend to help fix it in your memory. If you keep in mind what you and the Spirit are to do in each phase, you can cooperate more closely with the Spirit.

3. Make your own outlines of the B-I-R-T-H stages in the stories of Jesus' winning the Samaritan woman (John 4), Philip winning the Ethiopian official (Acts 8), and Peter winning Cornelius and his household (Acts 10).

4. Memorize the "ABC—Sacrifice, Savior, Lord" outline of the gospel from Session 14, along with the points under each main point. Without referring to any written source, write a sinner's prayer that includes the elements of the outline above. Compare it with the one you wrote in Session 14, and revise it until you are satisfied. Now commit it to memory in faith that you will be using it—soon!

5. Write out an up-to-date testimony to help you explain Christian living in practical terms.

   a. Focus primarily on your current relationship with Jesus. (You don't need a dramatic conversion experience or a bad past life to have a testimony worth sharing. If you do have those things, don't talk much about them. Instead, talk mostly about your present relationship with Jesus.)

   b. Use words that are understandable to an unchurched person, just as Jesus used everyday language and illustrations.

   c. Write a two-minute version and a five-minute version so you can be prepared for opportunities of varying time lengths.

6. Witness to a nonbelieving friend by reviewing your assignments with him or her. Be alert for the Holy Spirit's arranging other opportunities (bridges), and be conscious of His presence to help you while you are sharing. Also be alert to His working in the heart of your friends before, during, and after your sharing. In other words, tune into the F-L-O-W of the Spirit so you can do your part in bringing God's love to people. You can certainly depend on the Spirit to do His part.

7. By doing the **THRIVE** sessions with the help of a discipling friend, you have been preparing yourself to be a discipling friend to someone else in need. Winning someone to Christ and helping that new brother or sister establish his or her own contact and conduct with God is the most important reason for being alive.

❧ CONGRATULATIONS ☙

You have completed the **Thrive** sessions with the help of God and whoever else you have studied with. But your real spiritual foundations are still not in place unless you are actively involved in winning others to Christ and being a discipling friend to them. Never stop eagerly responding to God's loving presence by loving Him in return and by loving others in teamwork with Him. Be the best discipling friend to young believers and peer discipler to fellow believers that God can help you to be – encouraging each other and holding each other accountable for applying God's truth to your daily behavior!

May the Lord of the harvest send you daily into His harvest. "Go and make disciples… And surely [He is] with you always, to the very end of the age" (Matthew 28:19–20).

New Christian Life Materials
by James H. Hall

THRIVE

Discipler's Guide $20

- ☐ Gives complete instructions for one-to-one or small-group discipling of new Christians or for peer discipling for Christian growth
- ☐ Can be used individually for self-help instruction or for training disciplers
- ☐ New-Christian or peer discipling sessions included with answers and Discipler Helps

Handbook for New Christians $14

- ☐ Fifteen reproducible sessions for mentoring new Christians until they can win and mentor others
- ☐ Session worksheets guide new Christians to the milk of the Word, to learn how to live in daily conversation and cooperation with Jesus

Handbook for Christian Growth $15

- ☐ Fifteen sessions to facilitate growth for an individual Christian or for peer discipling teams – and also trains participants to win and mentor others
- ☐ Session worksheets guide individual Christians or peer disciplers to the written Word, to learn how to live in daily conversation and cooperation with Jesus
  (Includes assessments to identify spiritual strengths/weaknesses and spiritual gifts)

StartUp Studies .... $3/multiples $2.50 ea.

- ☐ Four lessons adapted from Sessions 1 and 2 in the *THRIVE* handbook for new Christians, plus guidelines for evangelism/discipling by the new believer (20 pages, 8.5 in. x 5.5 in.)

To order materials and/or schedule ministry

www.newchristian.com

Rev. James H. Hall, New Christian Life Ministries

1411 E. Stoneridge St. • Springfield, MO 65803

Phone: 417-833-9052 • Fax: 417-833-1142 • E-mail: JHHalls@aol.com

Shipping and handling: $1.00 to $49.99—15 percent; over $50—10 percent
Make checks payable to NCLM.

Credit card orders: www.newchristian.com

Testimonies

Since your seminar, I feel so much more confident now in bringing someone to the Lord. —J.M.

Thank you for these lessons. I now recognize that God loves me and is always with me. I rest in Him now because I don't worry much. I don't think of vengeance on others. I give it all to Jesus. —I.M.

The questions can be applied on a personal level, so the believer may come to know how powerful and real our Father is. My relationship with Him has definitely changed.... My Christian friend (discipler) is great. —F.L.

We began Bible studies in homes in the projects, using the *Harvester's Handbook* [now *THRIVE*]. A number of people gave their hearts to the Lord for the first time or recommitted their lives. —G.F.

The Lord is really using this workbook to reach souls at the Kokomo Rescue Mission. It made the love of Christ so clear to me that I wanted to share it. —M.C.

At pastor/care group leader meetings, I teach a lesson, then they teach it to their care group, and then members teach it to newcomers to our church. —D.W.

People learn to read the Bible, get confidence, develop relationships, free up in worship...so many areas of their lives are affected. —S.S.

People have become bolder and more outgoing in witness and in casual meetings of persons. —R.C.

When I accepted Jesus as my Savior, I wanted to serve Him and lead a Christian life, but I didn't know how. Your lessons clearly explained how I was to live. They are a wonderful tool for new converts. Now I'll be on the teaching end. Thanks again. —C.W.

Used in hundreds of churches nationwide!
More testimonies at
www.newchristian.com